PIANO • VOCAL • CHORDS

WORLD'S GREATEST
LOVE SONGS

50 of the Most Popular Love Songs Ever Written

This volume contains dozens of beautiful love songs that have endured over the decades. Included are great standards from the '20s and '30s such as "Embraceable You" and "I've Got You Under My Skin," as well as classic movie love themes such as "Laura," "Love Is a Many Splendored Thing," "The Rose," "True Love," "As Time Goes By," and "Somewhere, My Love."

You will also find songs from the modern era, including several made famous by today's superstars such as Josh Groban, Madonna, Michael Bublé, Richard Marx, Jim Brickman, and Faith Hill.

Alfred Publishing Co., Inc.
16320 Roscoe Blvd., Suite 100
P.O. Box 10003
Van Nuys, CA 91410-0003
alfred.com

ISBN-10: 0-7390-5123-7
ISBN-13: 978-0-7390-5123-8

Contents by Title

Contents by Decade

1980s

1990s

2000s

ANNIE'S SONG

Words and Music by
JOHN DENVER

A7
G
rain. Like a storm in the des -
A
Bm
G
D
D/C♯
ert, like a sleep - y blue o - cean,
Bm7
D/A
G
F♯m
Em
you fill up my sens - es, come
A7
D
Dsus
D
Dsus
fill me a - gain. Come let me

G A Bm G
love you, let me give my life
sens - es like a night in a
D D/C♯ Bm7 D/A G
to you. Let me drown in your laugh -
for - est, like the moun - tains in spring -
F♯m Em G A7
ter, let me die in your arms.
time, like a walk in the rain.
G A Bm
Let me lay down be - side you, let me
Like a storm in the des - ert, like a
(2nd time hold back…

G
D
D/C♯
Bm7
al - ways be with you.
sleep - y blue o - cean, you
…a tempo)
D/A
G
F♯m
Em
A7
Come let me love you, come love me a -
fill up my sens - es, come fill me a -
1.
D
Dsus
D
Dsus
2.
D
gain. You fill up my gain.
Dsus
D
Dsus
D
Dsus
D

AS TIME GOES BY

Words and Music by
HERMAN HUPFELD

G/D B7 Em B7 G7 Dm G7
must get down to earth, at times re - lax, re - lieve the ten - sion. No mat - ter what the pro - gress, or
C Em Am Dm Dm7/A Dm7(♭5)/A♭ Dm7/G G7
what may yet be proved, the sim - ple facts of life are such they can - not be re - moved. You
poco rit.
Refrain: Liltingly
Dm7 G7 Gm6 G7 C G+ C
must re - mem - ber this, a kiss is still a kiss, a sigh is just a sigh. The
p – mf
D7 G7sus G7 Dm G7 Cmaj7 C6 Cmaj7 C6
fun - da - men - tal things ap - ply, as time goes by. And

Dm7 G7 Gm6 G7 C G+ C
when two lov - ers woo, they still say, "I love you." On that, you can re - ly.
D7 Gsus G7 Dm7 G7 C F Fm
No mat - ter what the fu - ture brings, as time goes by.
C C7 F A7
Moon - light and love songs, nev - er out of date;
mf–f
cresc. poco a poco
Dm F♯dim7 Am F7
hearts full of pas - sion, jeal - ous - y, and hate. Wom - an needs man, and

D7
G7
Gdim7
G7
man must have his mate, that, no one can de - ny. It's
poco rit.
p – mf
Dm7
G7
Gm6
G7
C
G+
C
still the same old sto - ry, a fight for love and glo - ry, a case of do or die.
a tempo
D7
C
C♯dim7
The world will al - ways wel - come lov - ers, as
Dm7
G7
G7(♯5)
1. C
Am
D7
G7
2. C
B♭7
C
time goes by. You by.
f
mf
f
8vb

AT LAST

Lyric by
MACK GORDON
Music by
HARRY WARREN
Slowly, with expression
G7 C Am Dm7 G9 Dm7
At last, my love has come a -
mf
C Am Dm7 G7(♯5) G7 C Am7
long. My lone - ly days are o - ver
Dm7 Fm6 G7 C Am Dm7(♭5) G9
and life is like a song. At

C
Am
Dm7
G9
Dm7
C
Am
last,
the skies above are blue.
Dm7
G7(♯5)
G7
C
Am7
Dm7
Fm6
G7
My heart was wrapped in clo - ver the night I looked at
C
Fm
G7(♭9)
C
G7
C7
Fmaj7
G7(♭9)
you.
I found a dream that I can
Cmaj7
C6
B
F♯m7(♭5)
B7(♭9)
Em
speak to, a dream that I can call my own.
I found a

Am7(♭5) D7 Gmaj7 G6 Am7 D7(♭9) G Dm7/G G7
thrill to press my cheek to, a thrill I've nev - er known. You
C Am Dm7 G9 Dm7 C Am
smiled and then the spell was cast,
Dm7 G7(♯5) G7 C Am Dm7 G7(♭9) G7
and here we are in heav - en, for you are mine at
1. 2.
C Am F6 G7(♭9) G7 C6 Dm7(♭5) G7(♭9) C6
last. At last.
rit.

BEAUTIFUL
(As You)

Words and Music by
JIM BRICKMAN, JACK KUGELL
and JAMIE JONES

Slowly and freely ♩ = 60

B♭ Gm7 Cm7 F F/E♭

mf

(with pedal)

Dm7 E♭2 Fsus F

Verse:

B♭(9) Gm7 E♭2 F7sus F7

1. From the mo-ment I saw___ you, from the mo-ment I looked_ in-to___ your eyes,_
2. *See additional lyrics*

mp

B♭
Gm7
Cm7
F7sus
F7
there was some-thing a - bout you. I knew, I knew
B♭
Gm7
E♭2
F7sus
F/E♭
that we were once in a life - time, a trea-sure near im-pos - si-ble to find.
B♭/D
E♭2
F7sus
F7
And I know how luck - y I am to have you.
Chorus:
B♭(9)/D
E♭
F7sus
F7
F/E♭
'Cause I've seen rain - bows that could take your breath a - way,

B♭(9)/D Gm Cm7 F7 F/E♭

the beau-ty of the set - ting sun__ that ends a per - fect day.__

Dm7 E♭maj7 Gm F Em7(♭5)

And when it comes to shoot - ing stars,__ I have seen__ a few.________ But I've

Cm7 B♭/D E♭2 F7sus

nev - er seen__ an - y - thing__________ as beau - ti - ful__ as

1.

B♭ Gm Cm7 F7

you.

mf

2.
B♭
Gm
Cm7
F7
F7/E♭
you.
La da da da da da da.
mf
B♭(9)/D
E♭
F7sus
G7sus
Oh.
Chorus:
C(9)/E
F(9)
C/G
G
G/F
I've seen rain - bows that could take your breath a - way,
f
C(9)/E
Am7
Dm7
G
G/F
the beau - ty of the set - ting sun that ends a per - fect day.

Em7
Fmaj9
Am
G
F♯m7(♭5)
And when it comes to shoot - ing stars,
I have seen a few.
But I've
Dm7
C/E
F2
G7sus
nev - er seen an - y - thing,
oh, no, I've
mf
Em7
Am
Em/G
D9/F♯
nev - er seen an - y - thing
Fm
C
Am
as beau - ti - ful as you.
mp

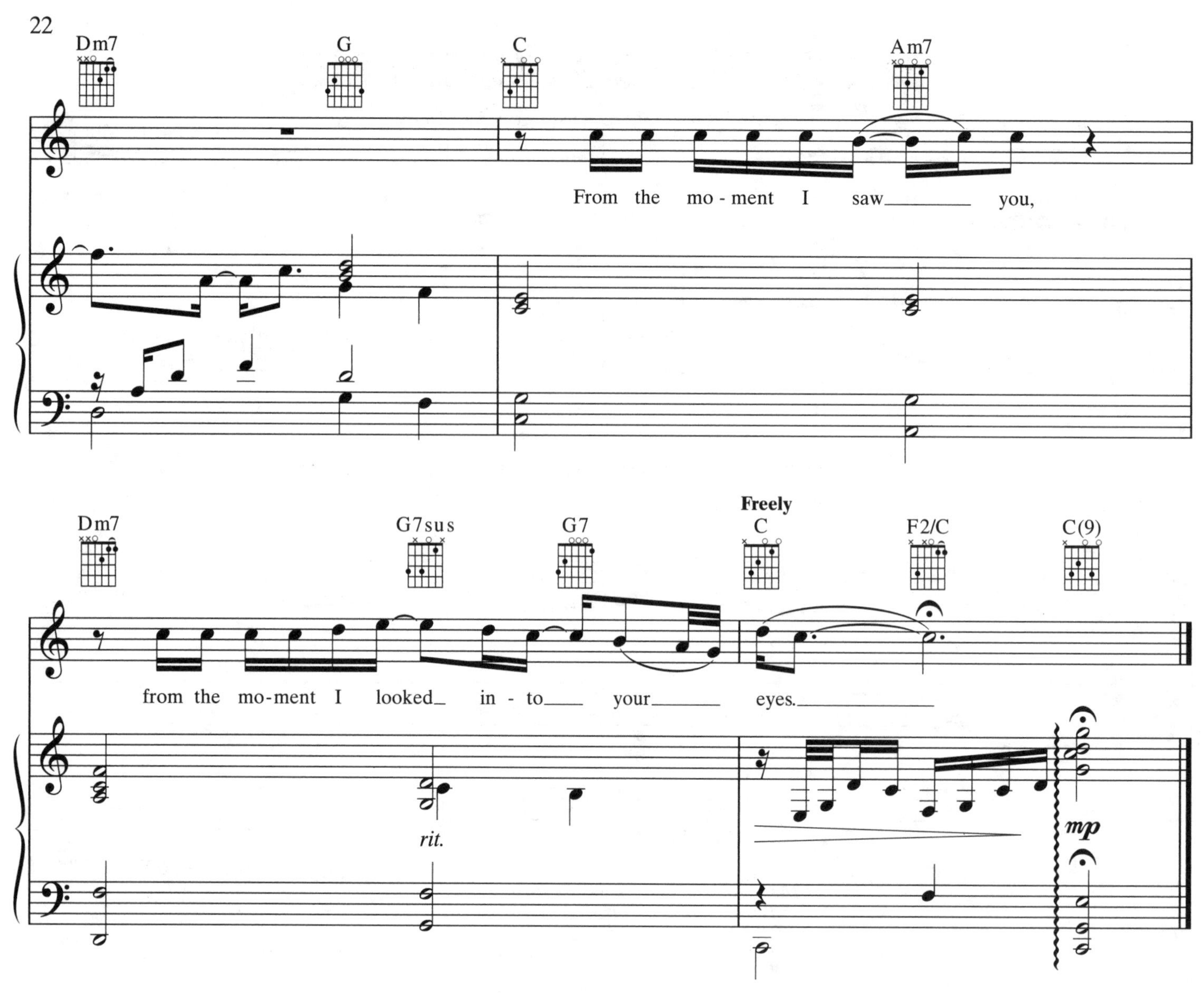

Verse 2:
Holding you in my arms,
No one else has fit so perfectly.
I could dance forever with you, with you.
And at the stroke of midnight,
Please forgive me if I can't let go,
'Cause I never dreamed I'd find
A Cinderella of my own.
(To Chorus:)

BECAUSE YOU LOVED ME

(Theme from *Up Close & Personal*)

Words and Music by
DIANE WARREN

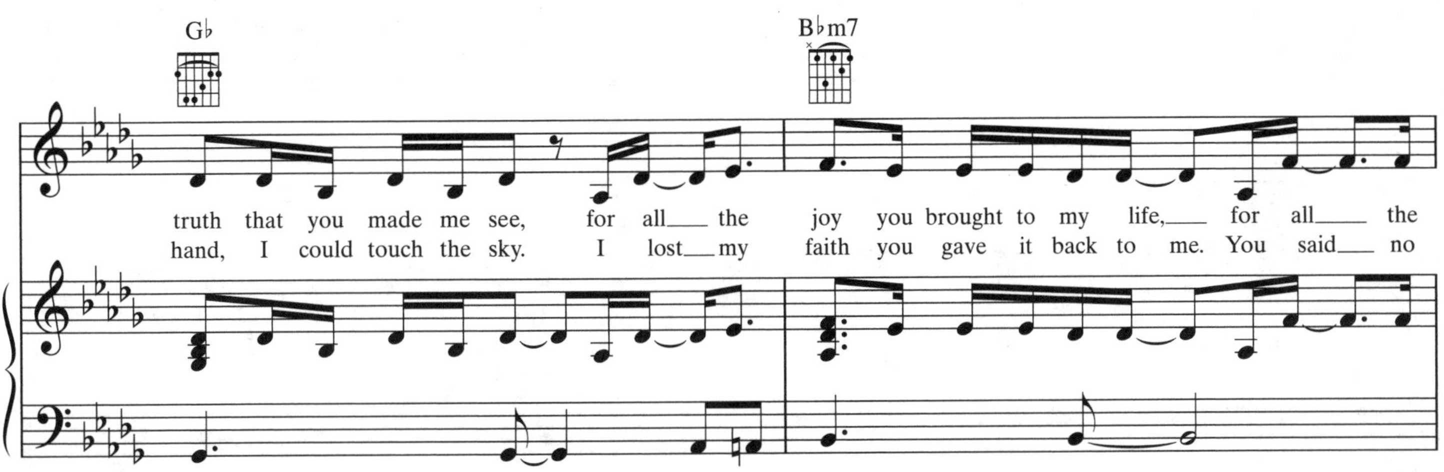

G♭maj7
E♭m7/A♭
love I found in you, I'll be for - ev - er thank - ful, ba - by.
love, I had it all. I'm grate - ful for each day you gave me.
C♭6
B♭m7
E♭m7
You're the one who held me up, never let me fall.
May - be I don't know that much, but I know this much is true.
G♭m7
E♭m7/A♭
You're the one who saw me through, through it all.
I was blessed be - cause I was loved by you.
You were my
Chorus:
D♭
G♭
strength when I was weak, you were my voice when I could-n't speak. You were my

B♭m7 A♭sus A♭

eyes when I could-n't see, you saw_ the best there was_ in me, lift-ed_ me_

Fm7 G♭maj9 C♭maj7

up when I could-n't reach. You gave_ me faith 'coz you_ be-lieved._ I'm

To Coda 𝄌 1.

E♭m7/A♭ D♭ E♭m7/A♭

ev-ery-thing_ I am be-cause_you loved_ me. 2. You gave_ me

2.

D♭

loved_ me.

Bridge:

F7/A B♭m7

You were al-ways there_ for me, the ten-der wind_ that car-ried_me. A

F7/A
B♭m7
light in the dark, shin - ing your love in - to my life. You've
E♭m7
D♭/F
been my in - spi - ra - tion, through the lies, you were the truth. My
E♭m7/A♭
D.S. 𝄋 al Coda
world is a bet - ter place be - cause of you. You were my
Coda D♭
Fm7/B♭
E♭
loved me. You were my strength when I was weak, you were my

A♭ Cm7

voice when I could-n't speak. You were__ my eyes when I could-n't see, you saw__ the

B♭sus Gm7

best there was__ in me, lift-ed__ me__ up when I could-n't reach. You gave__ me

A♭maj9 D♭maj7 Fm7/B♭

faith 'coz you__ be-lieved.__ I'm ev-ery-thing__ I am be-cause__ you

E♭ Fm7/B♭ E♭

loved__ me. I'm ev-ery-thing__ I am be-cause__you loved__ me.__

CAN YOU FEEL THE LOVE TONIGHT

(from Walt Disney Pictures' "The Lion King")

Lyrics by
TIM RICE

Music by
ELTON JOHN

E♭
Gm7
A♭
F
It's e - nough for this rest - less war - rior just to be with you. And
cresc.
B♭
F/A
Gm
E♭
can you feel the love to - night?
mf
B♭
E♭
C/E
F
E♭
B♭/D
It is where we are.
It's e - nough for this
Gm7
Gm7/F
E♭
Cm
B♭/D
E♭
C/E
wide - eyed wan - der - er that we got this far.

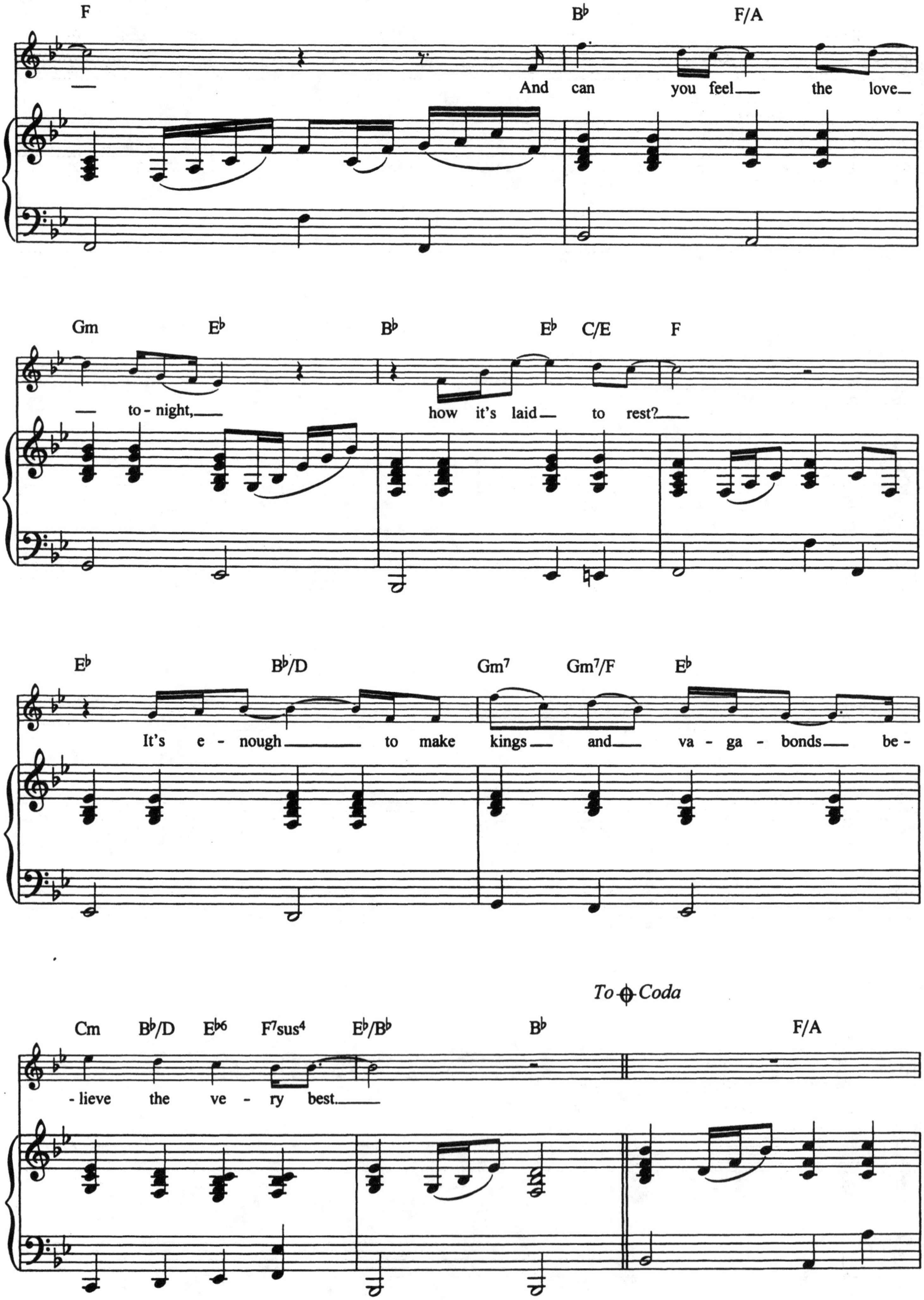

F B♭ F/A

And can you feel the love

Gm E♭ B♭ E♭ C/E F

tonight, how it's laid to rest?

E♭ B♭/D Gm7 Gm7/F E♭

It's e - nough to make kings and va - ga - bonds be -

E♭/G
B♭/F
E♭
B♭/D
F/A
B♭
Cm7
B♭
E♭
B♭/D
E♭
B♭/D
There's a time for ev - 'ry one, if they on - ly learn
mp
E♭
B♭/D
Cm7
F/A
that the twist - ing ka - lei - do - scope moves us all in turn.
E♭
B♭/D
E♭
B♭/D
There's a rhyme and rea - son to the wild out - doors

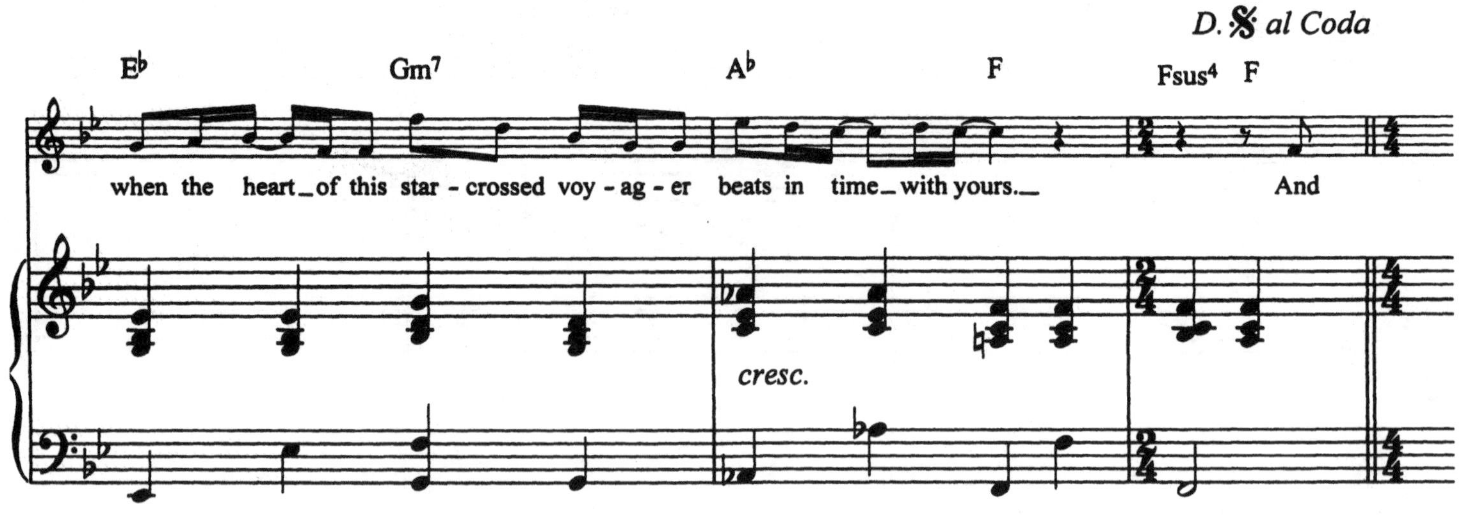
D.𝄋 al Coda
E♭
Gm7
A♭
F
Fsus4 F
when the heart_of this star-crossed voy-ag-er beats in time_with yours._
And
cresc.

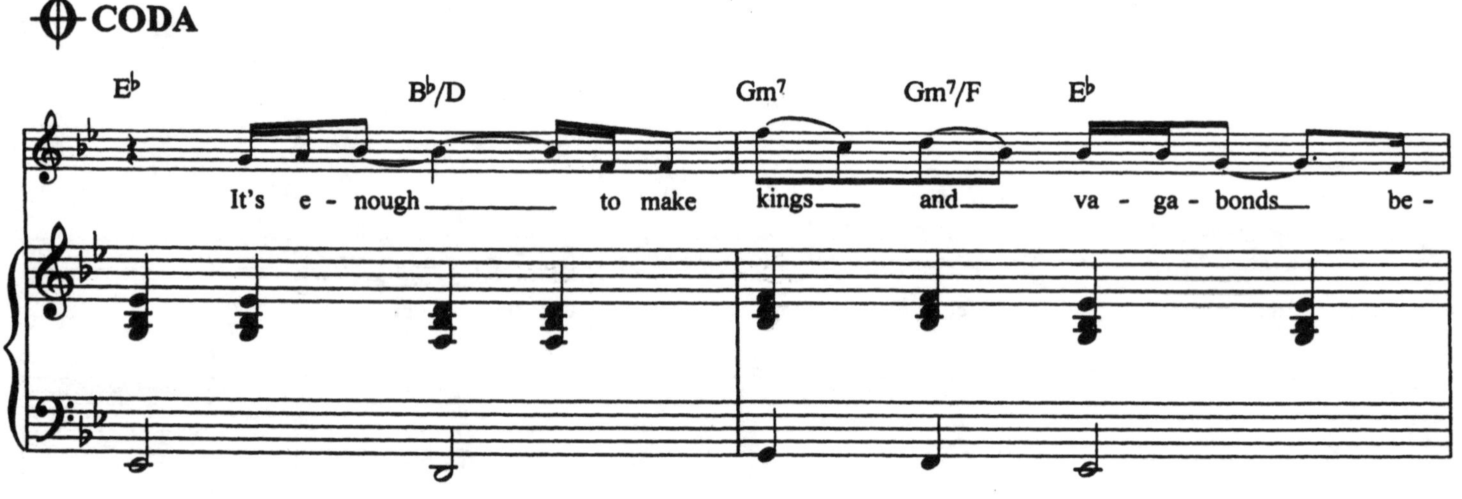
CODA
E♭
B♭/D
Gm7
Gm7/F
E♭
It's e-nough_ to make kings_ and_ va-ga-bonds_ be-

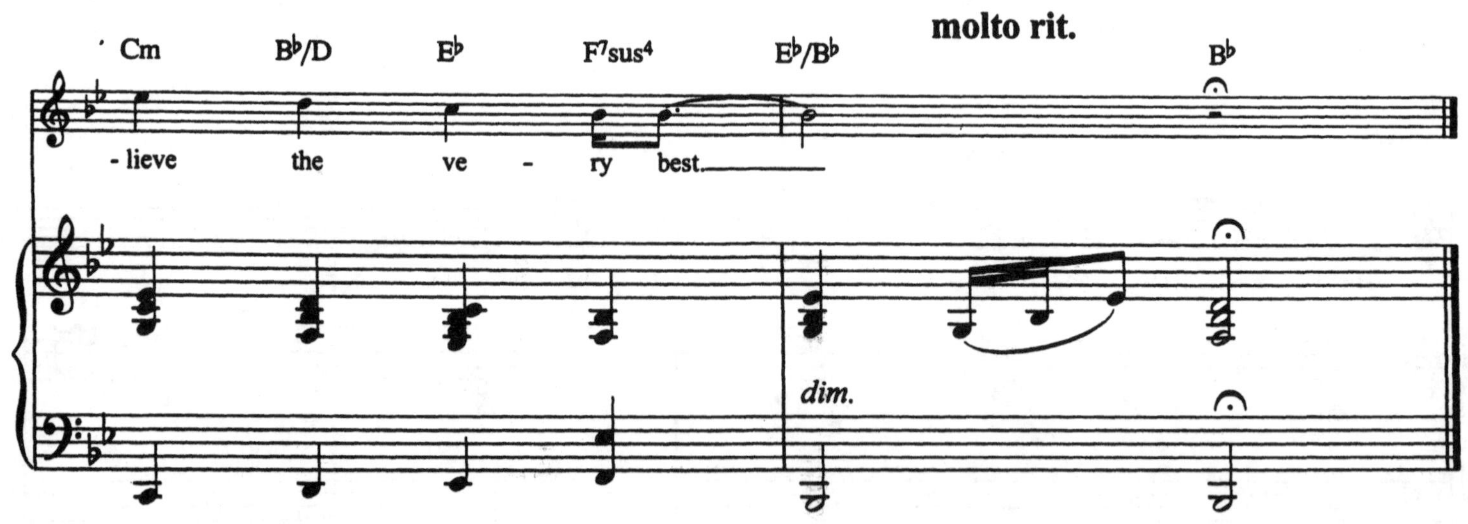
molto rit.
Cm
B♭/D
E♭
F7sus4
E♭/B♭
B♭
-lieve the ve-ry best._
dim.

CRAZY FOR YOU

Words and Music by
JOHN BETTIS and JON LIND

Esusus2
Asus2
Bsus4
Esus2
Two by two their bod - ies be - come one.
Eye to eye, we need no word at all.
Asus2
A/B
Esus2
Asus2
Bsus4
I see you through the smok - y air.
Slow - ly now we be - gin to move.
Esus2
Asus2
Bsus4
Esus2
Can't you feel the weight of my stare.
Ev - 'ry breath I'm deep - er in - to you.
You're so close, but still
Soon we two are stand
Asus2
G♯/B♯
C♯m
B/C♯
C♯m
4fr.
G/A
3fr.
A/B
a world a - way.
in' still in time.
What I'm dy - in' to say: You bet I'm
If you read my mind, you'll see I'm

Esus2 Esus2/G♯ C♯m7 4fr.

cra - zy for__ you. Touch__ me once__ and you'll know it's true.__

D6/E 7fr. Amaj9 Esus2/G♯

I nev - er want - ed an - y - one like this.__ It's all brand__ new.__ You'll

1. F♯m7 A/B Esus2

feel it in my kiss.__ I'm cra - zy for you,__

Asus2 Bsus4 Esus2 Asus2 A/B

cra - zy for____ you.____

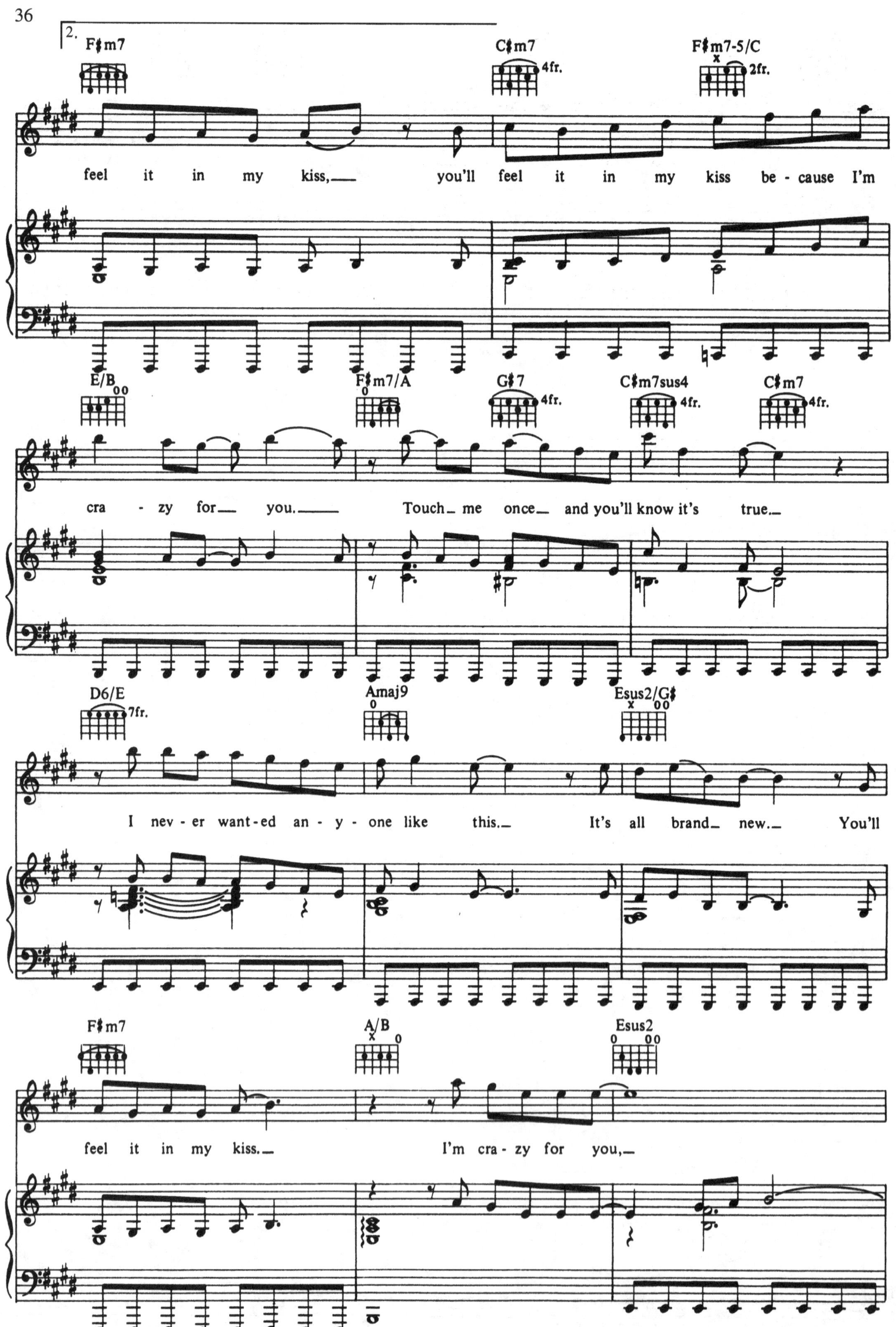
2.
F♯m7
C♯m7
4fr.
F♯m7-5/C
2fr.
feel it in my kiss, you'll feel it in my kiss be - cause I'm
E/B
F♯m7/A
G♯7
4fr.
C♯m7sus4
4fr.
C♯m7
4fr.
cra - zy for you. Touch me once and you'll know it's true.
D6/E
7fr.
Amaj9
Esus2/G♯
I nev - er want - ed an - y - one like this. It's all brand new. You'll
F♯m7
A/B
Esus2
feel it in my kiss. I'm cra - zy for you,

Asus2 Bsus4 Esus2 Asus2 Bsus4

cra - zy for ___ you, ___ cra - zy for you, ___

Esus2 Asus2 Bsus4 Esus2

___ *(Spoken)* *cra - zy for you.*

Asus2 A/B Esus2 Asus2 Bsus4

It's all brand new. ___ I'm cra - zy for you. ___

1. 2. *D.S.* 𝄋 *(vocal ad lib) and fade*

Esus2 Asus2 Bsus4 Asus2 A/B

___ And you know it's true. ___ I'm cra - zy, cra - zy for you. ___

EMBRACEABLE YOU

Music and Lyrics by
GEORGE GERSHWIN and IRA GERSHWIN

G
F#7
What was it that con - trolled me?
What kept my love - life
B
F#7
B
lean?
My in - tu - i - tion told me You'd come
Am7
G
Em A9 Em A9
on the scene.
La - dy, lis - ten to the rhy - thm of my
Em Em6 Em A7
Am D
Am D Am D Am D
rall. e dim.
heart - beat, And you'll get just what I mean.
rall. e dim.

Rhythmically
Refrain:
G C#o D7 Am11 Fm6 D7
Em-brace me, My sweet em - brace - a-ble you!
p-mf
Am F7 D7 G D7sus4 G
Em - brace me, You ir - re - place - a-ble you!
Em Em7 Em6 F#7 Bm Bb+ Bm7 E7
Just one look at you, my heart grew tip - sy in me;
D D#o A7 D7
You and you a - lone bring out the gyp - sy in me!

G
C♯o
D7
C
Fm6
D7
I love all the man - y charms a - bout you;
Am
F7
D7
G7
D7sus4
B♭m6
G7
C
A - bove all I want my arms a - bout you.
Don't be a
Am6
B7
Em
E♭+
G
Em6
G
naught - y ba - by, Come to pa - pa, Come to pa - pa, do! My sweet em -
L.H.
Cm6
D
1.
G
E♭
A
D7
2.
G
brace - a - ble you!
you!

EMILY

Words by
JOHNNY MERCER

Music by
JOHNNY MANDEL

Dreamily ♩ = 66

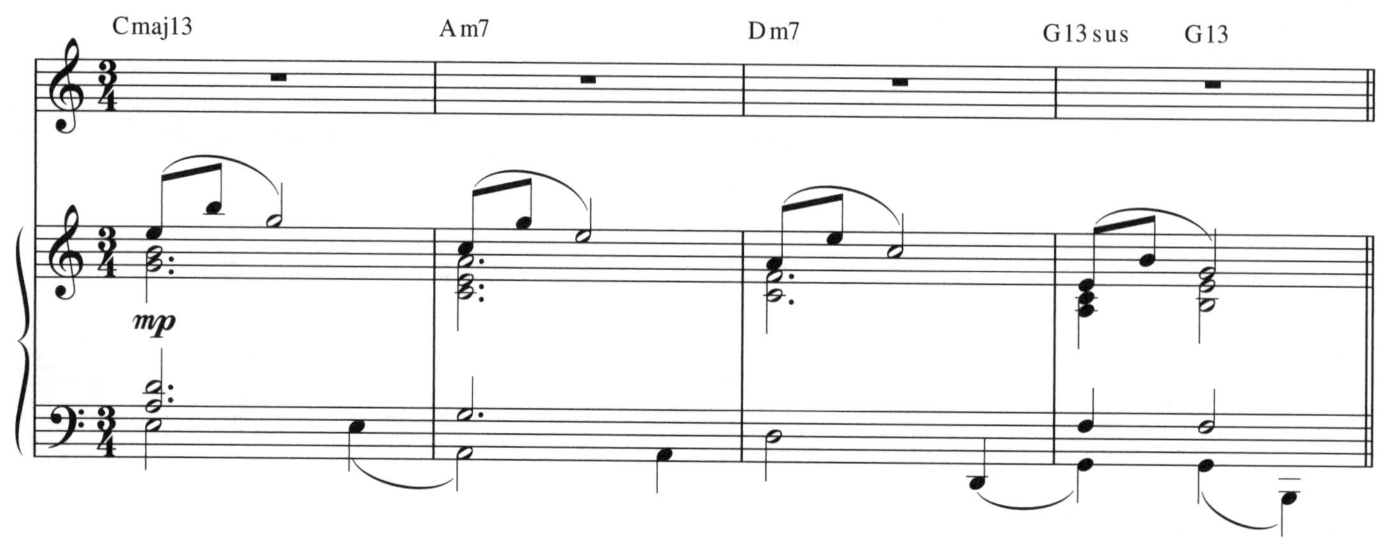

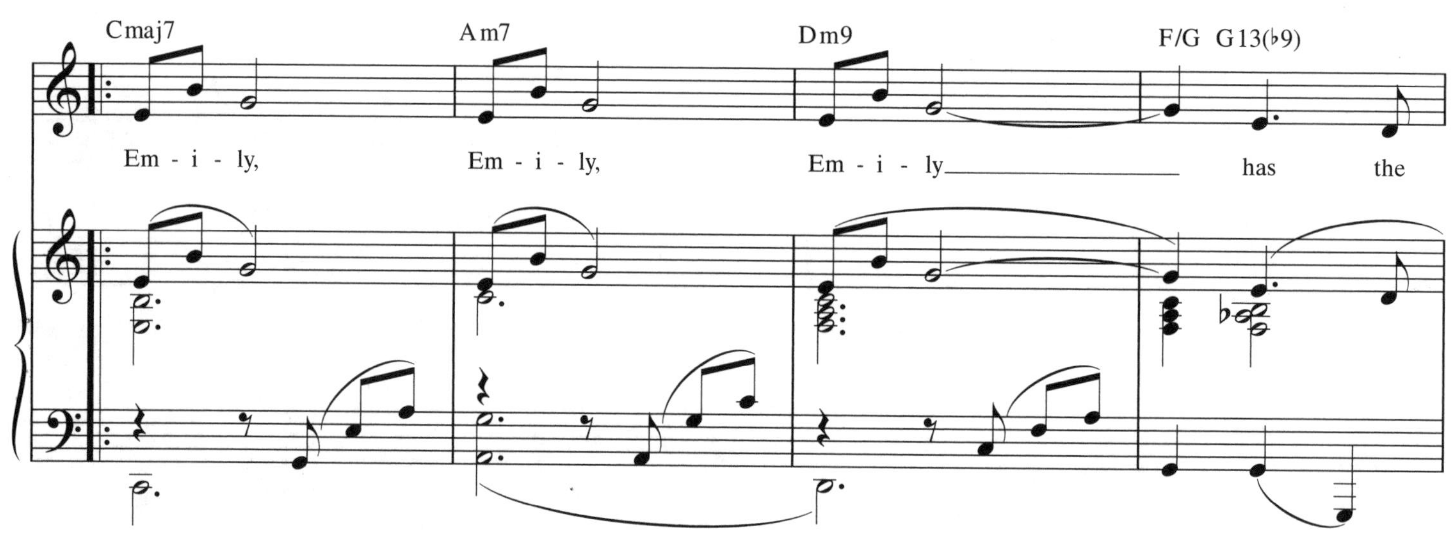

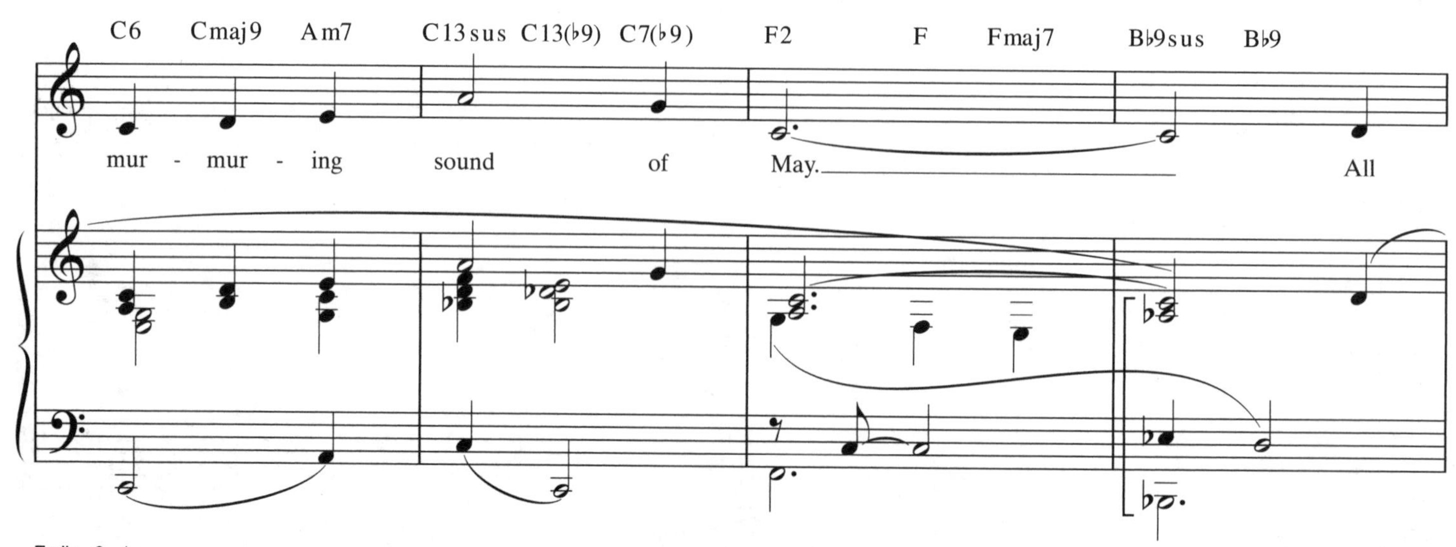

Emily - 3 - 1

C♯m7 A/C♯ F♯m7 Bm7 D/E E7(♭9)
sil - ver bells, cor - al shells, car - ou - sels and the
Am7 D9 Dm7/G G7(♭9 ♯5)
laugh - ter of chil - dren at play say
Cmaj9 Am7 Dm9 G13 G7(♭9 ♯5)
Em - i - ly, Em - i - ly, Em - i - ly and we
Cmaj9 Am7 C7sus C9 C7(♯5) Fmaj7 F6 Fmaj7 Bm7 E13(♭9)
fade to a mar - vel - ous view. Two

Am Bm/A Am7 B7(♭9 ♯5) B7(♭9) Em7 A13 C♯dim7
lov - ers a - lone and out of sight see - ing
Dm7 G13 G7(♯5) Em7 B♭13 A9 Dm7 G7/D Dm7
im - a - ges in the fire - light. As my eyes vis - ual -
Fm9(♯5) Fm6/9 Fm7 Em7 A9 A7(♭9 ♯5) Dm9 G13 G7(♯5)
ize a fam - i - ly, they see dream - i - ly, Em - i - ly
1. 2.
C2 G13sus E♭6 D♭maj7 C2 C6/9
too. too.
8vb

ENDLESS LOVE

Words and Music by
LIONEL RICHIE

E♭
E♭/F
Fsus
F
you're ev - 'ry breath that I take,
you're ev - 'ry
I'll hold you close in my arms,
I can't re -
B♭
F/A
E♭
step I make.
And I,
sist your charms.
And, love,
mf
E♭/F
F
B♭
F/A
Gm
Dm/F
I want to share all my love
I'll be a fool for you I'm
E♭
E♭/F
F
B♭
with you,
no one else will do.
sure;
you know I don't mind.

B♭9
E♭
E♭/F
F
And your eyes,
they tell me how
'Cause you,
you mean the
B♭
F/A
Gm
F6
E♭
much
you
care.
Oh,
yes,
you will
world
to
me.
Oh,
I know
Dm7
Cm7
E♭/F
al - ways be
my end - less
I've found you
my end - less
8va
1.
B♭
love.
mp

2.
B♭
E♭
E♭/F
Fsus
F
love.
mp
Bum,
bum,
bum, bum, bum,
bum,
bum,
bum,
bum,
bum,
bum, bum,
bum.
Oh,
and,
love,
cresc.
mf

Eb/F
F
Bb
F/A
Gm7
F/A
I'll be that fool for you I'm
Eb
Eb/F
F
Bb
sure; you know I don't mind.
Bb9
Eb
Eb/F
F
And yes, you'll be the
Bb
F/A
Gm
Dm/F
Ebmaj7
on - ly one. No one can de - ny

Dm7
Ebmaj7
Dm7
this love I have in - side. I'll
Ebmaj7
Dm7
Cm7
give it all to you my love, my love,
Eb/F
Bb
my end - less love.
p
Eb
Eb/F
Fsus
Bb
Eb/Bb
Bb
rit.

EVERYTHING

Words and Music by
MICHAEL BUBLÉ, ALAN CHANG
and AMY FOSTER-GILLIES

D Bm7 E7 G G/A
ming pool on an Au - gust day, and you're the per - fect thing to say.
ter - y, you're from out - er space, you're ev - 'ry min - ute of my ev - 'ry
D A7sus D Bm7 E7
And you play it coy, but it's kind of cute, ah, when you
day. And I can't be - lieve, ah, that I'm you're man, and I
Gm A7sus D A7sus D Bm7
smile at me, you know ex - act - ly what you do. Ba - by, don't pre - tend that you don't know
get to kiss you, ba - by, just be - cause I can. What - ev - er comes our way, ah, we'll see
E7 Gm A7sus D
it's true. 'Cause you can see it when I look at you.
it through, and you know that's what our love can do.
And in this cra -

Chorus:

G A D Bm7 G A

zy___ life,___ and through these cra - zy times,_

D D7 G F♯7(♭9) Bm D/A

___ it's you,___ it's you.___ You make me sing.___ You're ev - 'ry line,_

E7 Gm Em7(♭5)/A 1. D Bm7

___ you're ev - 'ry word,___ you're ev - 'ry - thing.___

E7 Gm Em7(♭5)/A D A7sus

2. You're a car -

2.
D
Bm7
E7
Gm
Em7(♭5)/A
D
(Inst. solo ad lib....
Bm7
E7
Gm
Em7(♭5)/A
D
...end solo) So
Bm7
E7
Gm
Em7(♭5)/A
D
la la la la la la la. So
Bm7
E7
Gm
A7(♭9)
D N.C.
la la la la la la la. And in this

Chorus:
Amaj7
B
E
C♯m7
A
B
cra - zy life, and through these cra - zy times,
E
E7
A
G♯7
C♯m
E/B
it's you, it's you. You make me sing. You're ev - 'ry line,
F♯7
Am6
C♯m
C♯m7/B
you're ev-'ry word, you're ev-'ry - thing.
3
F♯7
You're ev - 'ry song, and I sing a-long,

Am6
F♯m7(♭5)/B
E
C♯m7
'cause you're my ev - 'ry - thing.
F♯7
A
A/B
E
C♯m7
So la la
F♯7
Am
F♯m7(♭5)/B
E
la la la la la. So
Freely
C♯m7
F♯7
Am
E
la la la la la la la la la la la.

(EVERYTHING I DO) I DO IT FOR YOU

Words and Music by
BRYAN ADAMS, ROBERT JOHN "MUTT" LANGE
and MICHAEL KAMEN

Dbsus2
Ab/Db
Gb
Db/Ab
Ab
4fr.
soul, _ and when you find me there you'll _ search _ no more. Don't
life, _ I would give it all, I would sac - ri - fice. Don't
Ebm
Dbm
Ebm
Db/Eb
Ebm
Db
6fr.
tell me it's not worth fight - ing for. You can't tell me it's not worth dy - ing
tell me it's not worth fight - ing for. I can't help it, there's noth - ing I want
Ebm
Db
Absus4
for.
more.
You know it's true, _ ev - 'ry - thing I do, I do it for _
1. Db5
2. Db
Dbsus4
Db
you.
you. There's

Cb
Fb
Cb
Gb
no love like your love, and no oth - er could give more love. There's
Db
Ab
Eb
Ab
Absus4
4fr.
no way, un - less you're there all the time, all the way, yeah.
Gb(addAb)
Db
Gb(addAb)
Db

Ebm
6fr.
Ab
4fr.
Absus4
4fr.
Ab
4fr.
Oh, you can't tell me it's not worth try - ing for. I can't
Ebm
6fr.
Ab
4fr.
Db
4fr.
Dbsus4
4 fr.
Db
4 fr.
help it, there's noth-ing I want more. Yeah, I would fight for you, I'd
Ab
4fr.
Absus4
4 fr.
Ab
4 fr.
Gb
Gbm
lie for you, walk the mile for you, yeah, I'd die for you. You know it's
a tempo
Db/Ab
4fr.
Absus4
4fr.
Ab
4fr.
Gb
Gb6
x
Db
4fr.
true, ev-'ry - thing I do, oh, oh, I do it for you.
rit.

THE GIFT

Words and Music by
JIM BRICKMAN and
TOM DOUGLAS

Gm7
B♭/F
E♭(9)
B♭/D
Cm7
You're the an-swer when I prayed_ I would find some - one, and, ba - by, I___ found you._
Chorus:
F7sus
F7
B♭/D
E♭(9)
F7sus
F7
___ And all I want___ is to hold___ you for - ev - er.___ And all I need_
B♭/D
E♭(9)
F7sus
F7
B♭/D
D7
___ is you more___ ev - 'ry day.___ You saved my heart___ from be - ing
Gm
B♭/F
Em7(♭5)
Cm7
B♭/D
F7sus
bro - ken a - part.___ You gave your love a - way, and I'm thank - ful ev-'ry day for the

B♭(9) F/A Gm7 B♭/F E♭(9)
gift.
Verse 2:
F(9) C/E Dm7 F/C B♭(9) F/A
He:
2. Watch-ing as you soft - ly sleep. What I'd give if I could keep just this mo-ment. If
Gm7 F(9) C/E Dm7 F/C
on - ly time stood still. But the col - ors fade a-way and the years will make us gray.
B♭(9) F/A Gm7 C7sus C7
Both:
But, ba - by, in my eyes, you'll still be beau-ti - ful. And all I want

Chorus:
F/A B♭(9) C7sus C7 F/A B♭(9)
__ is to hold__ you for - ev-er. All I need__ is you more__ ev - 'ry
C7sus C7 F/A A7 Dm F/C Bm7(♭5)
To Coda
He: She:
day. You saved__ my heart from be-ing bro-ken a - part.__ You gave__ your
Gm7 F/A C7sus F
He: Both:
love a - way, and I'm thank - ful ev-'ry day for the gift.
B♭(9) C7sus Dm7 F/A B♭(9) F/A Gm7 C7sus C7

D.S. 𝄋 al Coda
Bb(9)/D
C/E
F
Bb
Gm7
F/A
C7sus
C7
And all I want
Coda
Dm
F/C
Bm7(b5)
She:
Gm7
F/A
He:
bro - ken a - part.
You gave your love a - way.
I can't find the
Bb(9)
C/D
Dm7
Gm7
C7sus
F(9)
C/E
She:
Both:
words to say.
And I'm thank - ful
ev - 'ry day
for the
gift.
rit.
a tempo
Dm7
F/C
Bb(9)
C7sus
F(9)
rit.

HOW DEEP IS YOUR LOVE

Words and Music by
BARRY GIBB, MAURICE GIBB
and ROBIN GIBB

Fm7/B♭
E♭
Gm7
Cm7
And the mo - ment that you wan-der far from me, I wan-na
You're the light in my deep-est, dark - est hour. You're my
Na na na na na na na na na na na na na
Fm7
Fm7/B♭
A♭maj7
feel you in my arms a - gain. And you come to me on a sum-
Sav - iour when I fall. And you may not think I care
na na na na na na. And you come to me on a sum-
Gm7
Fm7
mer breeze, keep me warm in your love, then you soft -
for you, when you know down in - side that I real -
mer breeze, keep me warm in your love then you soft -
D♭9
Gm7
A♭maj7/B♭
ly leave.
ly do.
ly leave.
And it's me you need to show; how deep is your love.
How deep

Chorus:
E♭
E♭maj7
A♭maj7
is your love, how deep is your love? I really mean to learn.
A♭m6
E♭
B♭m/A♭
'Cause we're living in a world of fools, breaking us
C7
Fm7
1.2.
A♭m6
down when they all should let us be. We belong to you and me.
3.
A♭m6
E♭
Gm7
A♭maj7/B♭
D.S. and fade
to you and me. Na na na na na. How deep

I BELIEVE IN YOU AND ME

Words and Music by
SANDY LINZER and DAVID WOLFERT

B
Bmaj7
D♯m7/G♯
G♯m7
D♯m7
you will al-ways be the one___ for me.___ Oh, yes, you will.__
C♯m7 C♯m7/F♯
B
B/A
___ And I be-lieve in dreams a-gain.___ I be-lieve that love will nev-er end.__ And
E(9)/G♯
Em7
A9
B/F♯
like the riv-er finds___ the sea,__ I___ was lost,___ now I'm__
D♯m7
G♯m7
C♯m7
C♯m7/F♯
1.
B
C♯m7/F♯
N.C.
free, 'cause I be-lieve__ in you__ and__ me. 2. I will nev-er leave

2.
Bridge:
B
D♯m7
G♯m7
D♯m7
G♯m7
me.
May-be I'm a fool to feel the way I do.
mf
C♯m7
C♯m(maj7)
C♯m7
C♯m7/F♯
N.C.
Dm7/G
I would play the fool for-ev-er just to be with you for-ev-er. 3. I be-lieve in
Verse 3:
C
C/B♭
Fmaj9
mir-a-cles, and love's a mir-a-cle. And yes, ba-by, you're my dream come true.
Fm7/B♭
A♭/B♭
B♭/A♭
Fmaj7
C/G
Em7
Am7
I was lost, now I'm free, oh ba-by, 'cause

Verse 2:
I will never leave your side,
I will never hurt your pride.
When all the chips are down,
I will always be around,
Just to be right where you are, my love.
Oh, I love you, boy.
I will never leave you out,
I will always let you in
To places no one has ever been.
Deep inside, can't you see?
I believe in you and me.
(To Bridge:)

I COULD NOT ASK FOR MORE

Words and Music by
DIANE WARREN

Moderately slow rock ♩ = 66

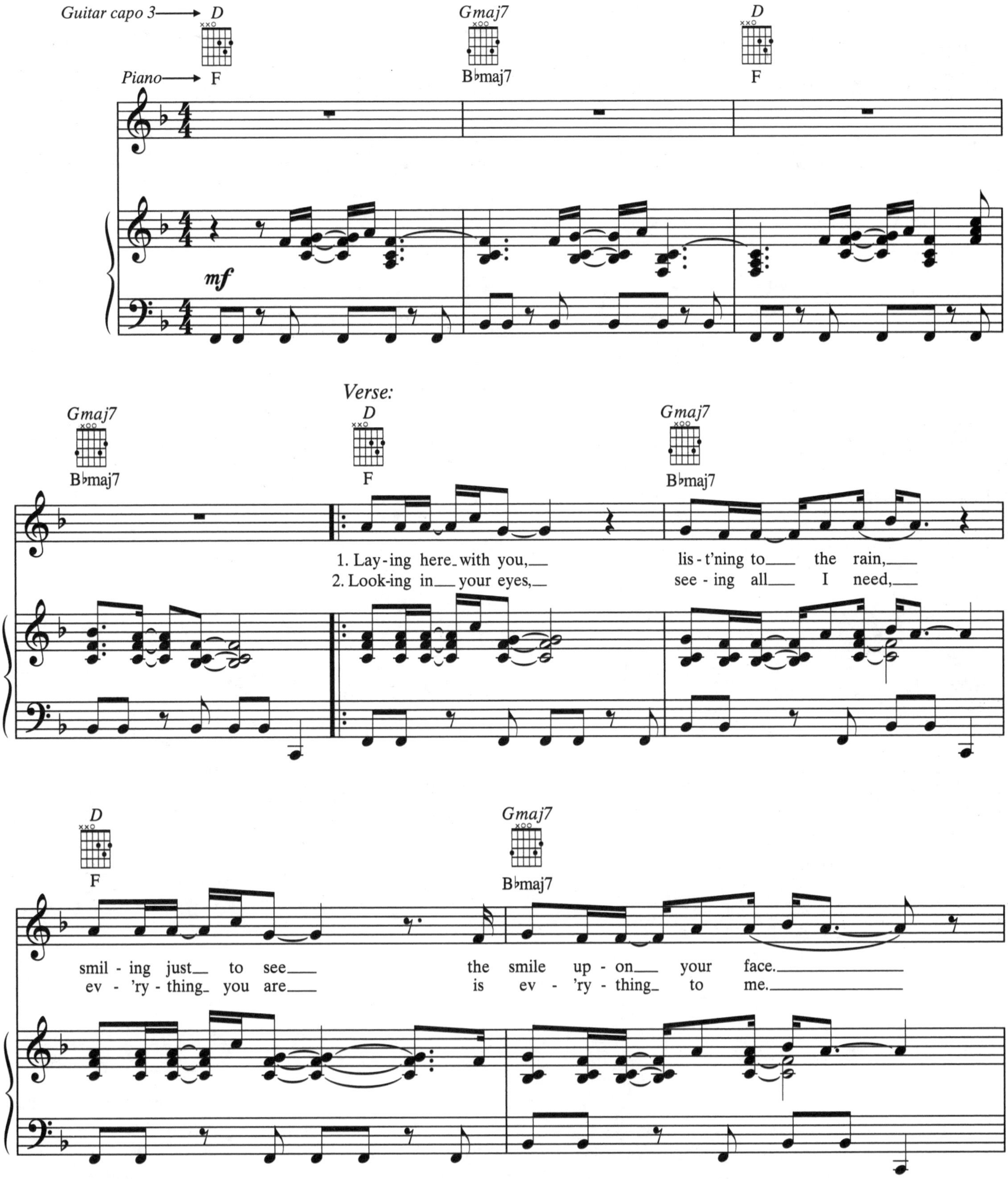
Guitar capo 3
Piano
D
F
Gmaj7
B♭maj7
D
F
mf
Gmaj7
B♭maj7
Verse:
D
F
Gmaj7
B♭maj7
1. Lay-ing here with you, lis-t'ning to the rain,
2. Look-ing in your eyes, see-ing all I need,
D
F
Gmaj7
B♭maj7
smil-ing just to see the smile up-on your face.
ev-'ry-thing you are is ev-'ry-thing to me.

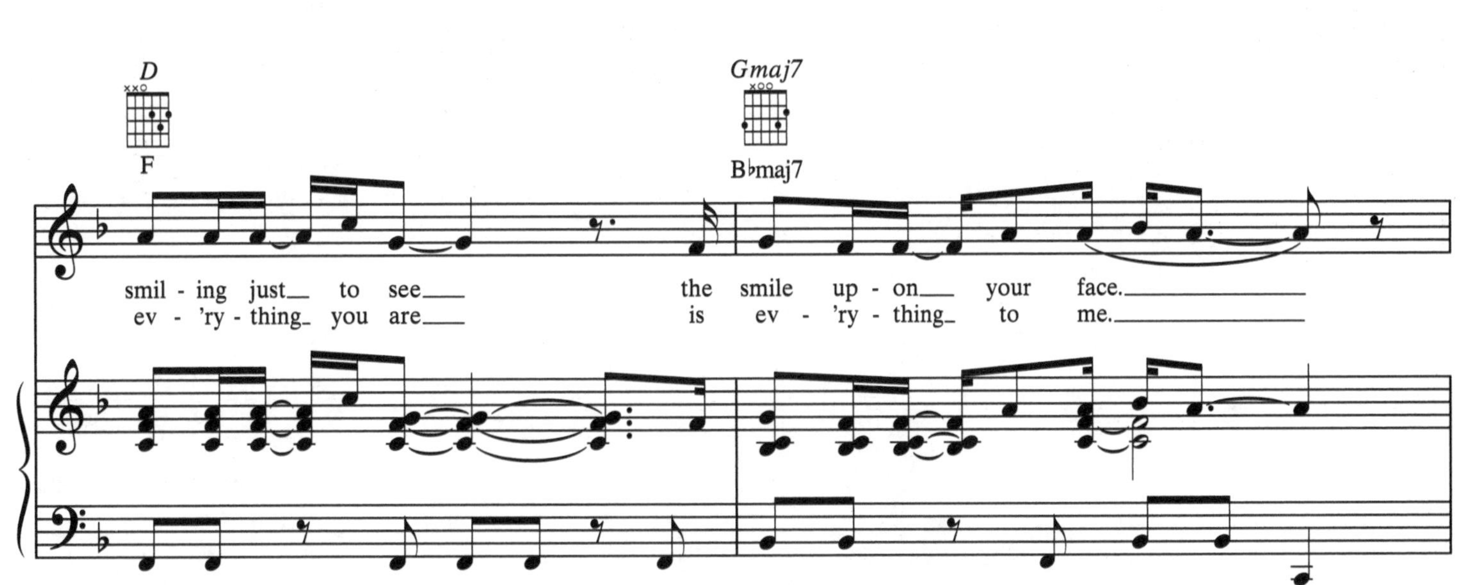

F♯m7
Am7
G
B♭
G/A
B♭/C
(1.3.) These are the mo - ments I thank God that I'm a - live.
(2.) These are the mo - ments I know heav - en must ex - ist.
F♯m7
Am7
Bm7
Dm7
E7
G7
These are the mo - ments I'll re - mem - ber all my life.
These are the mo - ments I know all I need is this.
(1.) I found
(2.) I have
(3.) I've got
Em7
Gm7
G
B♭
G/A
B♭/C
1.
D
F
all I've wait - ed for
and I could not ask for more.
Gmaj7
B♭maj7
2.3.
Dsus
Fsus
I could not ask for
cresc.

Chorus:
Gmaj7
B♭maj7
D
F
more than this time to - geth - er. I could not ask for more than this time with you. Ev - 'ry
f
C
E♭
G/B
B♭/D
A sus
Csus
prayer I have's been an - swered and ev - 'ry dream I have's come true. And
G2
B♭2
D
F
Dm/F
Fm/A♭
Dm
Fm
To Coda
right here in this mo - ment is right where I'm meant to be. Oh, here with you, here with
A sus
Csus
A
C
A sus
Csus
A
C
D
F
me, oh.
dim.
mf

Gmaj7
D
Gmaj7
D.S. 𝄋 al Coda
B♭maj7
F
B♭maj7
Coda
A sus
Csus
G2
B♭2
me.
I could not ask for
more_ than the love you give_ me,
'coz it's
D/F♯
Em7
Em7/A
D
F/A
Gm7
Gm7/C
F
all I've wait-ed for
and I could not ask for more,
oh,
dim.
mf
G2
D
Gmaj7
Repeat ad lib. and fade
B♭2
F
B♭maj7
ah,
oh
yeah.
And I could not ask for more..

From Touchstone Pictures' ARMAGEDDON

I DON'T WANT TO MISS A THING

Words and Music by
DIANE WARREN

G
D/F♯
Em7
smile while you are sleep - ing, while you're far a - way and dream - ing. I could
D
A/C♯
Bm7
G
D/F♯
spend my life in this sweet sur - ren - der. I could stay lost in this mo-ment for -
Em7
F♯m7
Gmaj7
Asus
ev - er. Ev-'ry mo-ment spent with you is a mo-ment I treas - ure.
Chorus:
D
A/C♯
Em7
Don't wan - na close my eyes, don't wan - na fall a - sleep, 'coz I'd

G A D A/C♯

miss you, ba-by, and I don't wan-na miss a thing.___ 'Coz e-ven when I dream of you,___

Em7 G A *To Coda*

the sweet-est dream would nev-er do.___ I'd still miss you, ba-by, and I don't wan-na miss a thing.___

D A/C♯ Bm7

2. Lay-ing

Verse 2:

D A/C♯ Bm7

close to you,___ feel-ing your___ heart beat-ing, and I'm

G
D/F♯
Em7
won - d'ring what you're dream - ing, won-d'ring if it's me you're see - ing. Then I
D
A/C♯
Bm7
kiss your eyes_ and thank God we're to - geth - er.___ I just wan - na
F♯m7
Gmaj7
Asus
D.S. 𝄋 al Coda
stay with you___ in this mo-ment for - ev - er, for - ev - er and ev - er.___
Bridge:
Coda
D
C
___ I don't wan - na miss one smile;___ I don't wan - na

G/B
B♭
miss one kiss. I just wan-na be with you, right here with you,
F/A
C
just like this. I just wan-na hold you close, feel your heart so
G/B
Dm7
close to mine, and just stay here in this moment for all the
3
Asus
A
rest of time. Ba - by, ba - by.

Chorus:
D
A/C♯
Em7
Don't wan-na close_ my eyes,_ don't wan-na fall_ a-sleep,_ 'coz I'd
G
A
D
A/C♯
miss you, ba-by, and I don't wan-na miss a thing._ 'Coz e-ven when I dream of you,_
Em7
G
A
the sweet-est dream would nev-er do._ I'd still miss you, ba-by, and I don't wan-na miss a thing._
D
A/C♯
Em7
_ Don't wan-na close_ my eyes,_ don't wan-na fall_ a-sleep,_ 'coz I'd

G
A
Bm7
A/C♯
miss you, ba - by, and I don't wan-na miss a thing.___ 'Coz e - ven when I dream of you,___
Em7
G
A
the sweet-est dream would nev - er do.___ I'd still miss you, ba - by, and I don't wan-na miss a thing.___
D
A/C♯
Em7
G
A
Repeat ad lib. and fade
D
A/C♯
Em7
G
A

I ONLY HAVE EYES FOR YOU

Words by
AL DUBIN

Music by
HARRY WARREN

Moderato

A7(♯5) Dm7 Dm7(♭5) G7 C6 G7 G7(♯5)

mf

poco rit.

C Am7 Dm7 Dm7(♭5) G7 C D7 G7(♯5)

My love must be a kind of blind love,

mp
tenderly

C Am7 Dm7 Dm7(♭5) G7 C D7 B7

I can't see an - y - one but you.

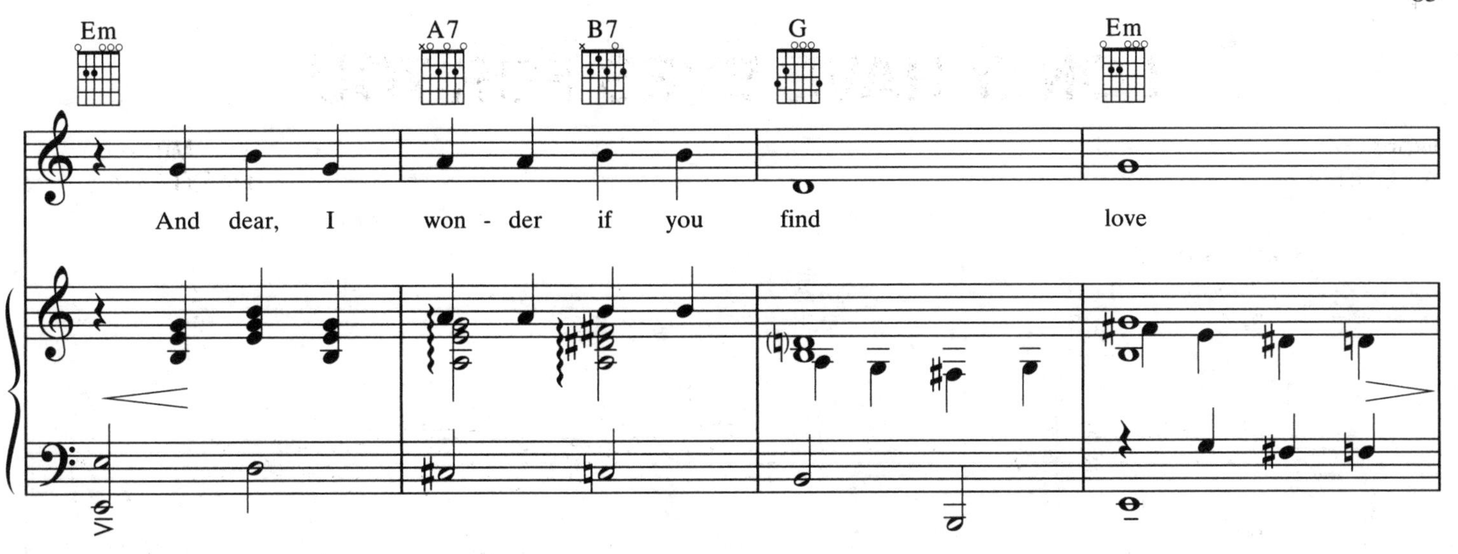
Em
A7
B7
G
Em
And dear, I won - der if you find love

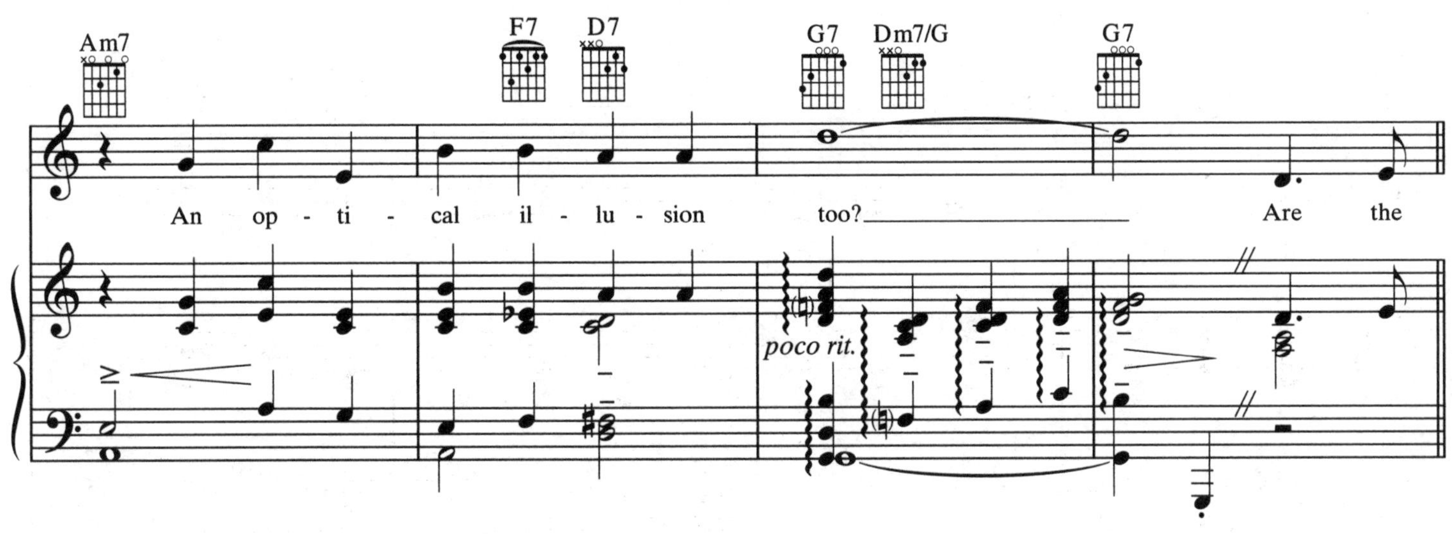
Am7
F7
D7
G7
Dm7/G
G7
An op - ti - cal il - lu - sion too? Are the
poco rit.

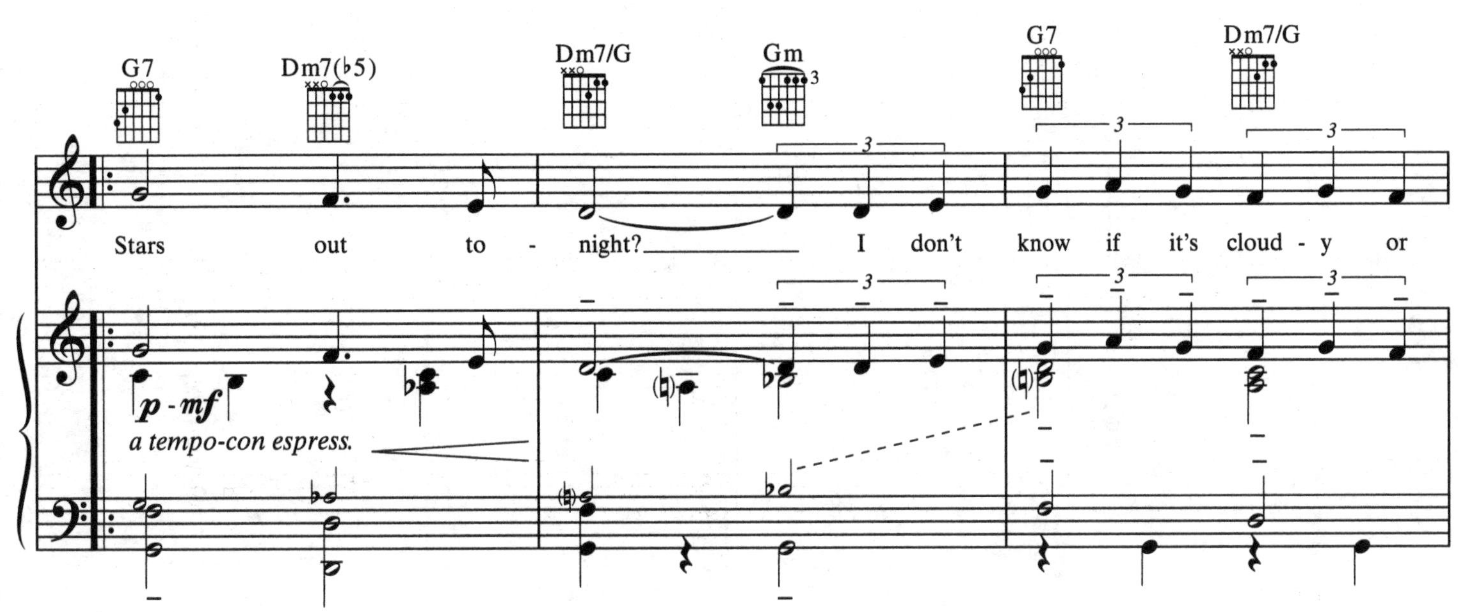
G7
Dm7(♭5)
Dm7/G
Gm
G7
Dm7/G
Stars out to - night? I don't know if it's cloud - y or
p - mf
a tempo-con espress.

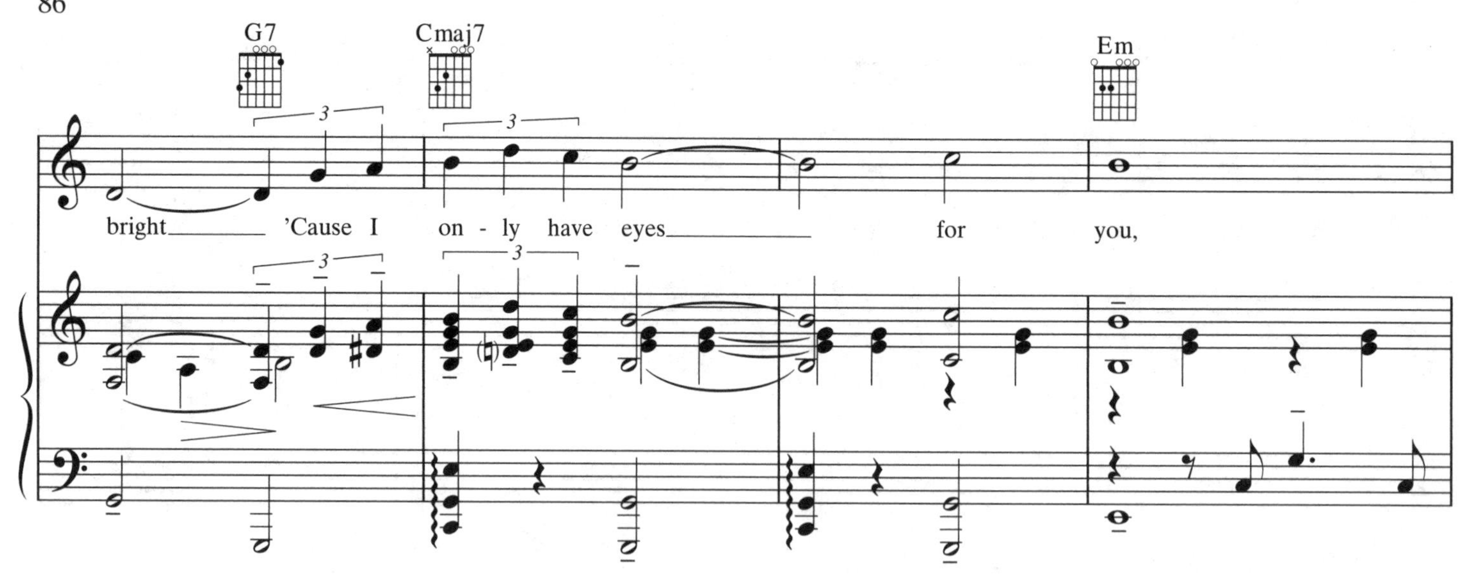
G7
Cmaj7
Em
bright 'Cause I on - ly have eyes for you,

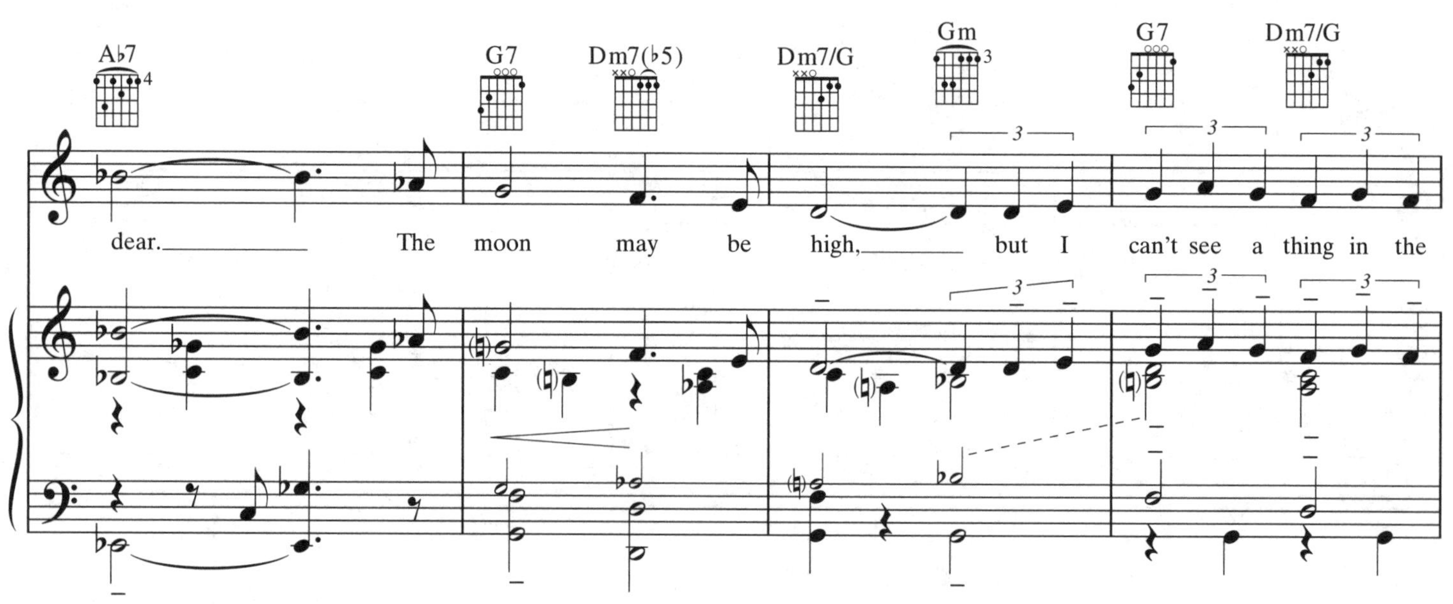
A♭7
G7
Dm7(♭5)
Dm7/G
Gm
G7
Dm7/G
dear. The moon may be high, but I can't see a thing in the

G7
Cmaj7
A7
sky, 'Cause I on - ly have eyes for you.

Dm7
G7
C
How can I live a day with - out you?
I don't know if we're in a gar - den,

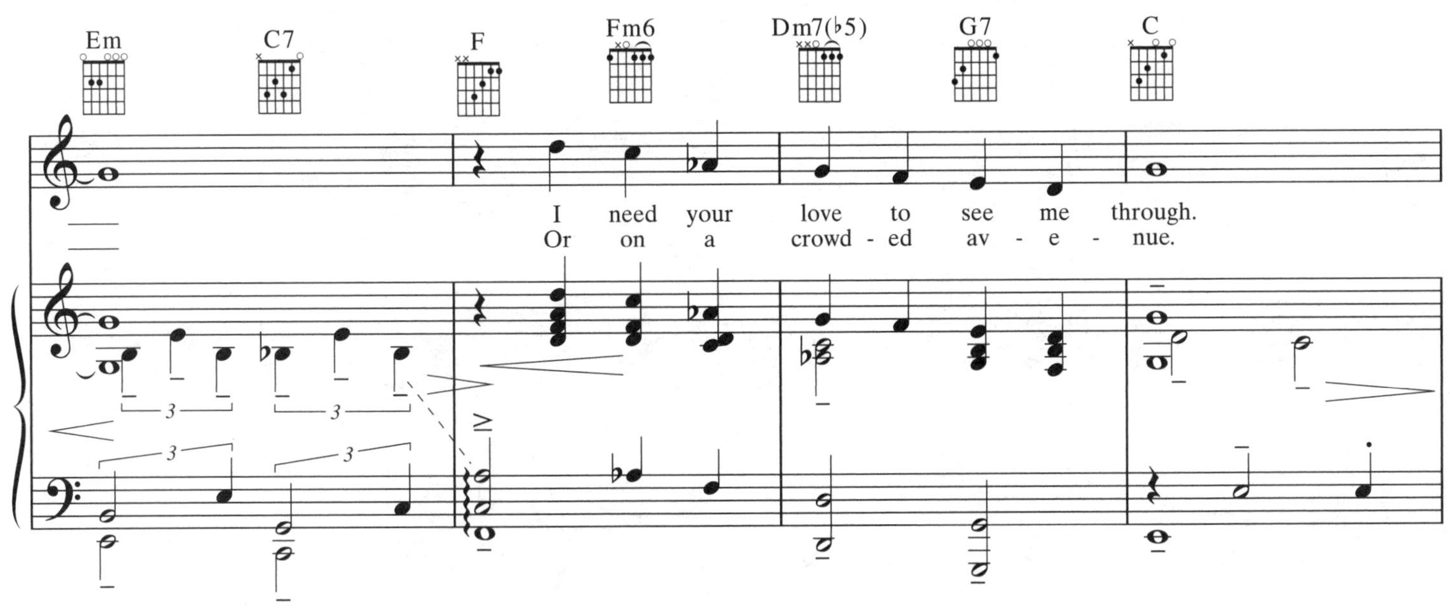
Em
C7
F
Fm6
Dm7(♭5)
G7
C
I need your love to see me through.
Or on a crowd - ed av - e - nue.

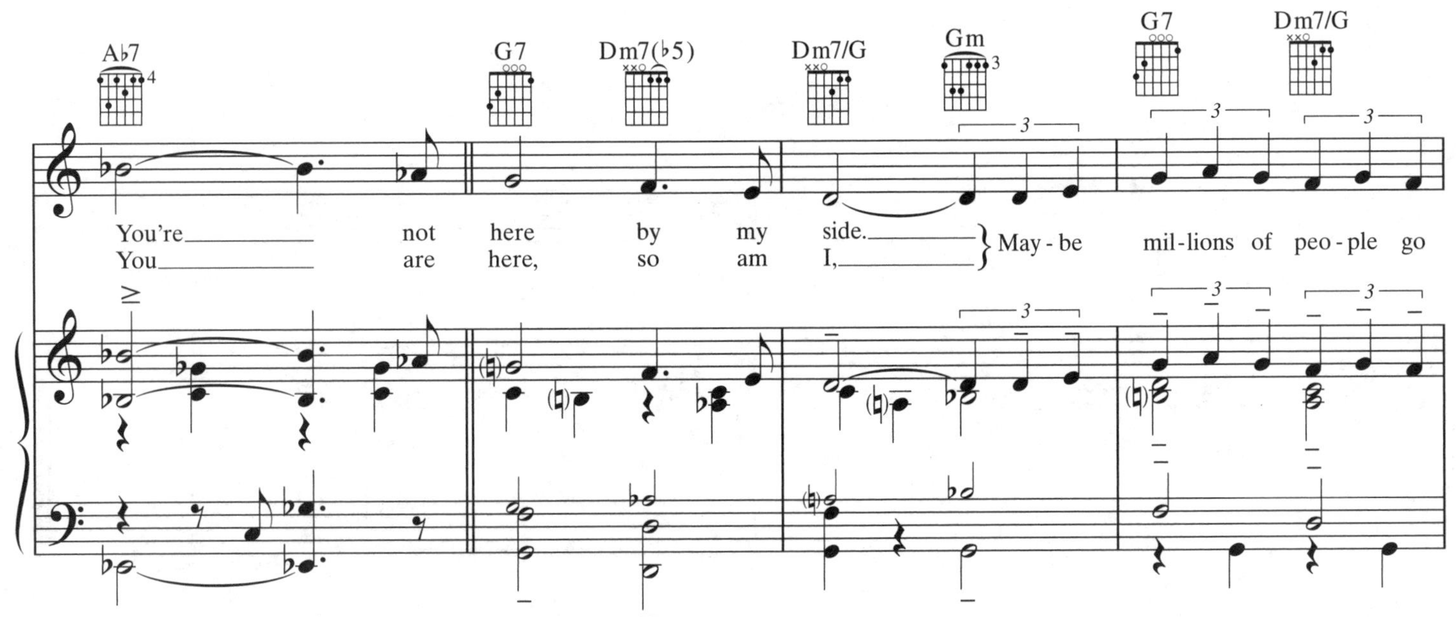
A♭7
G7
Dm7(♭5)
Dm7/G
Gm
G7
Dm7/G
You're not here by my side.
You are here, so am I,
May - be mil - lions of peo - ple go

G7
Cmaj7
by, But they all dis - ap - pear from

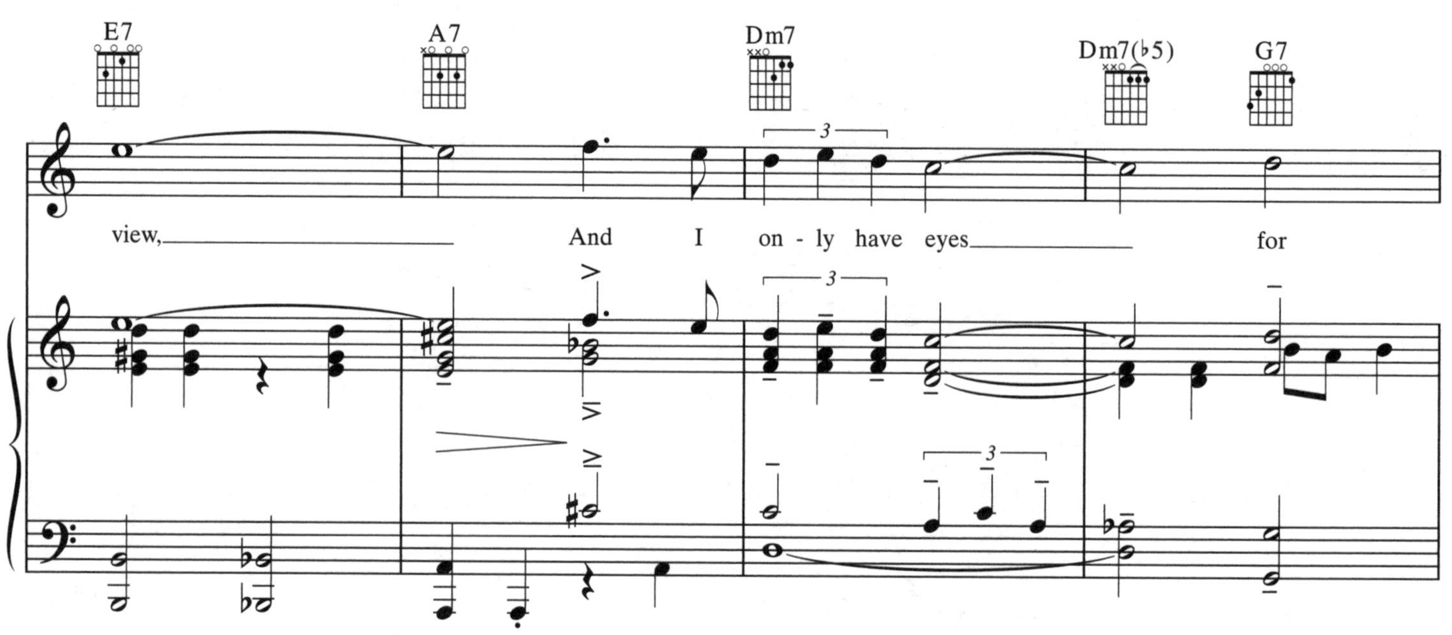
E7
A7
Dm7
Dm7(♭5)
G7
view, And I on - ly have eyes for

1.
2.
C
G7
C
C6
you. Are the you.
poco rit.

I'LL STAND BY YOU

Words and Music by
BILLY STEINBERG, TOM KELLY
and CHRISSIE HYNDE

G2
Bm
A
through, 'cause I've seen the dark side, too.
F♯m
Bm
F♯m
Bm
When the night falls on you, you don't know what to do, noth-ing you con -
G2
Asus
A
fess could make me love you less. I'll stand by
Chorus:
D
Bm7
you, I'll stand by you. I won't let no - bod - y hurt

Am
D
F
G
you,
I'll
stand
by
you.
Verse 2:
C
Em
2. So,
if you're mad,
get
mad,
don't hold it all in-
F2
G
G/B
side.
Come on and talk to
me
now.
C
Am7
Em
Hey,
what've you got to
hide?
I get an-gry,

F2
Am
G
too. Well, I'm a lot like you. When you're stand-
Em
Am
Em
Am
ing at the cross-roads and don't know which path to choose, let me come a-
F2
Gsus
G
long, 'cause e-ven if you're wrong, I'll stand by
Chorus:
D
Bm7
you, I'll stand by you. I won't let no-bod-y hurt

Am
D
you,
I'll stand by
you.
Take me in in - to your
Bm7
Am
To Coda
dark - est ho - ur,
and I'll nev - er de - sert
you.
I'll stand by
D
Bm7
G2
you.
Bm
A
And

F♯m
Bm
F♯m
Bm
when, when the night falls on you, ba - by, you're feel - ing all a -
G2
Asus
A
D.S. 𝄋 al Coda
lone, you won't be on your own. I'll stand by
⊕ Coda
D
Bm7
Asus
G
you. Oh, I'll stand by
D
Bm7
A
G
D
you. I'll stand by you.
molto rit.

IT HAD TO BE YOU

Words by
GUS KAHN

Music by
ISHAM JONES

It Had to Be You - 3 - 1

D7
D♯dim7
Em
could make me be blue,
A7
and e - ven be glad just to be sad thinking - ing of you.
D7
E♭7(♭5)
D7
D+
G
D+
Some oth - ers I've seen
G
E7
might nev - er be mean, might nev - er be cross

A7
or try to be boss,
but they would-n't do.
Am
Am7/G
F♯dim7
D7
For no-bod-y else
gave me a thrill.
With all your faults,
G
B7
Em
B♭dim7
D7
B♭dim7
D7
I love you still.
It had to be you,
won-der-ful you,
had to be you.
1.
G
B♭dim7
Am7(♭5)
D7
D+
2.
G
Cm6
G6
It had to be you.

I'VE GOT YOU UNDER MY SKIN

Words and Music by
COLE PORTER

Fm7 B♭7 E♭maj.7 E♭6
got you under my skin. I
Fm7 B♭7 E♭maj.7 E♭6
tried so not to give in, I
A♭m6 B♭7 D E♭maj.7 E♭6
said to my-self, "This af - fair nev-er will go so well." But
Dm7 G7 D♯dim. C
why should I try to re - sist when, dar-ling, I know so well I've
p
mf
marcato

Ab6
Abm
Bb7
Ebmaj. 7
Eb6
got you under my skin. I'd
Fm7
Bb7
Eb
Eb7
poco a poco cresc. ed appassionato
sac-ri-fice an-y-thing, Come what might, for the sake of hav-ing you near, In spite of a
poco a poco cresc. ed appassionato
Ab
Abm
Eb
Bb7
molto cresc.
warn-ing voice that comes in the night And re-peats and re-peats in my ear: "Don't you
subito p
molto cresc.
Cm
f molto espressivo
Ab
Bb7
Eb
Ebdim.
know, lit-tle fool, you nev-er can win, Use your men-
f molto espressivo

Fm7
Bb7
Eb
Bb+
Eb
mf
-tal - i - ty, Wake up to re - al - i - ty." But each
mf
Ab
cresc.
Abm
Eb
p rit
Bbm
C7
Guitar tacet
time I do, just the thought of you makes me stop, Be-fore I be - gin, 'Cause I've
cresc.
p rit
p dolce
Fm
Bb7(9b)
Eb
1.
a tempo
poco rit
got you un-der my skin. I've
a tempo
rit
ppp a tempo
poco rit
2. Fm7
Bb7
Eb
Bb7
Eb
poco rall.
più rall.
R.H.
morendo
ppp
8

LAURA

Lyric by
JOHNNY MERCER

Music by
DAVID RAKSIN

Andante

A13(♭9) Am7 D9

mf

G/D Gdim7/D Am7(♭5)/D

poco rall.

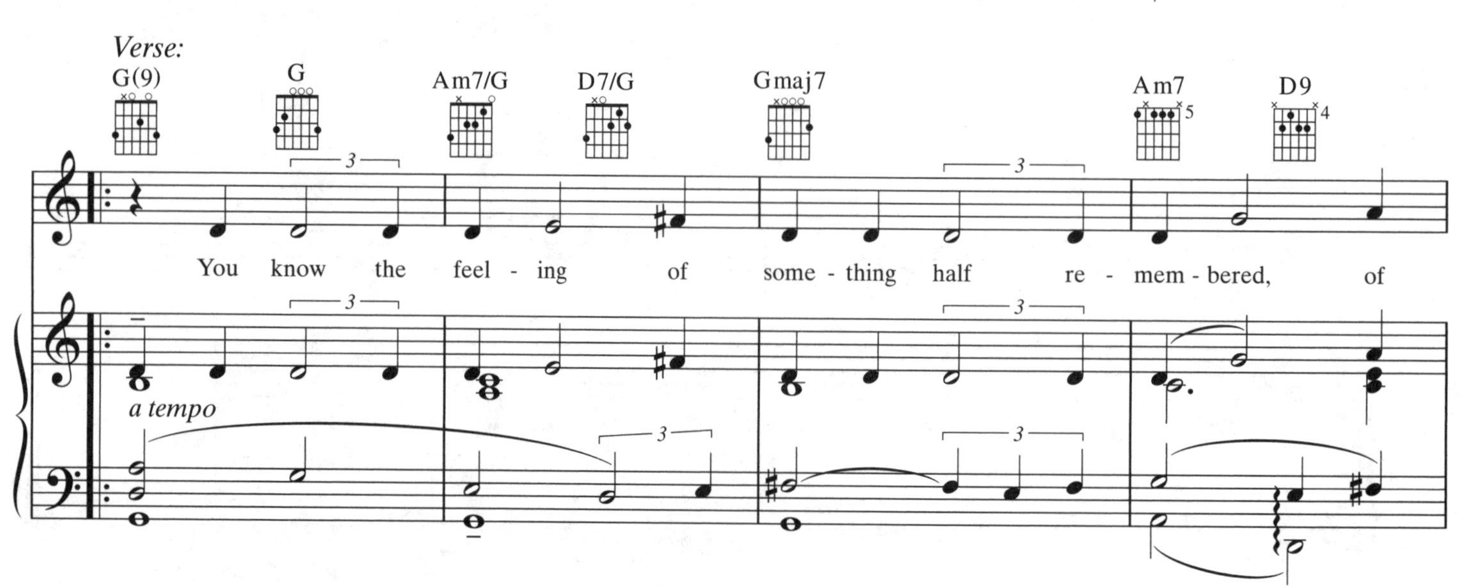

G(9)
G
G♯dim7
E7
Am7
D9
something that nev - er hap - pened. Yet you re - call it well.
B♭/D
D♭dim7
Cm7
C♭9
B♭(9)
Gm7
Em7(♭5)
A7(♯5)
You know the feel - ing of rec - og - niz - ing some - one that
poco ten.
A6/9
A7(♯5)
Am7/D
B♭m7/E♭
E♭7
you've nev - er met, as far as you could tell; well:
poco dim.
mp

Moderato
Chorus:
Am9
D7(♭9 ♯5)
Gmaj9
G6
Lau - ra is the face in the mist - y light,
mf
Gm9
C7(♭9 ♯5)
Fmaj9
F6 9
foot - steps that you hear down the hall.
Fm7
B♭7sus
B♭7
E♭maj7
E♭6
The laugh that floats on a sum - mer night that you can

Am7(♭5) D7(♭9/♭5) D9(♭5) D9 Bm7 E7(♭9/♯5)

nev - er quite ___ re - call. ___ And you see

poco rall.

Am9 D7(♭9/♯5) Gdim7 Gmaj13

Lau - ra ___ on the train that is pass - ing through. ___

a tempo

Gm9 C7(♭9/♯5) Fdim7 F6/9

Those eyes, ___ how fa - mil - iar they seem. ___

Fm7
Fm6
C6/9
D9
She gave your ver - y first kiss to you, that was
D7(♭9)
Dm7
Dm7/G
1.
C(9)
A13(♭9)
Dm9
E7(♭5)
E7
Lau - ra, but she's on - ly a dream.
2.
C(9)
A13(♭9)
Dm9
E7(♭5)
Am(9)
D♭/F
Fm6
G9sus
C(9)
dream.
rit.

LET'S DO IT
(Let's Fall In Love)

Words and Music by
COLE PORTER

Moderate swing, slighty rubato ♩ = 92

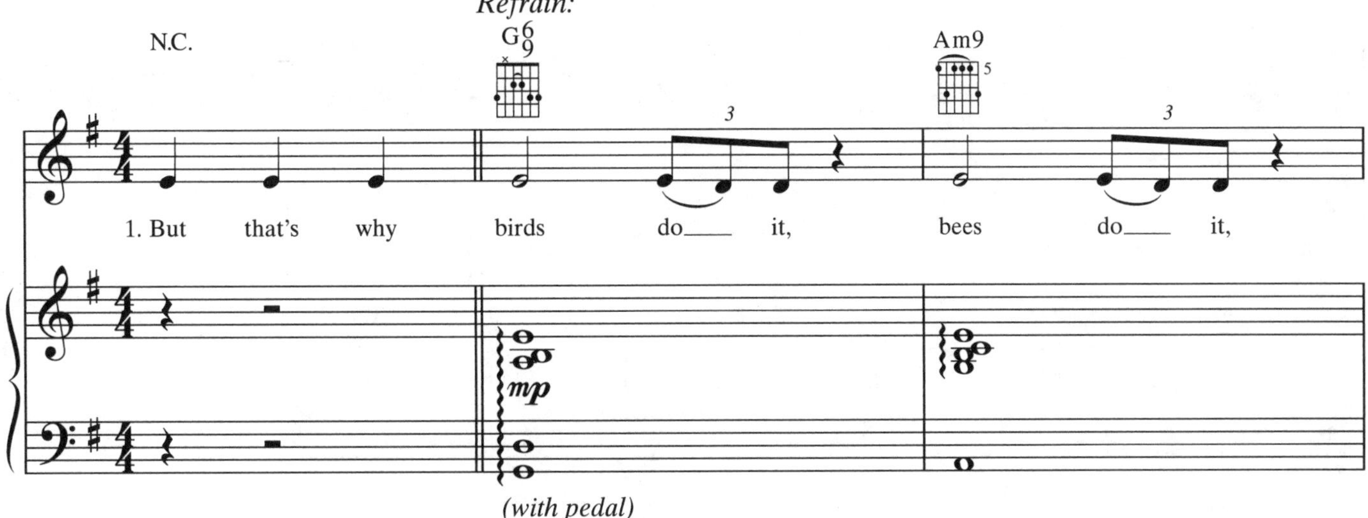

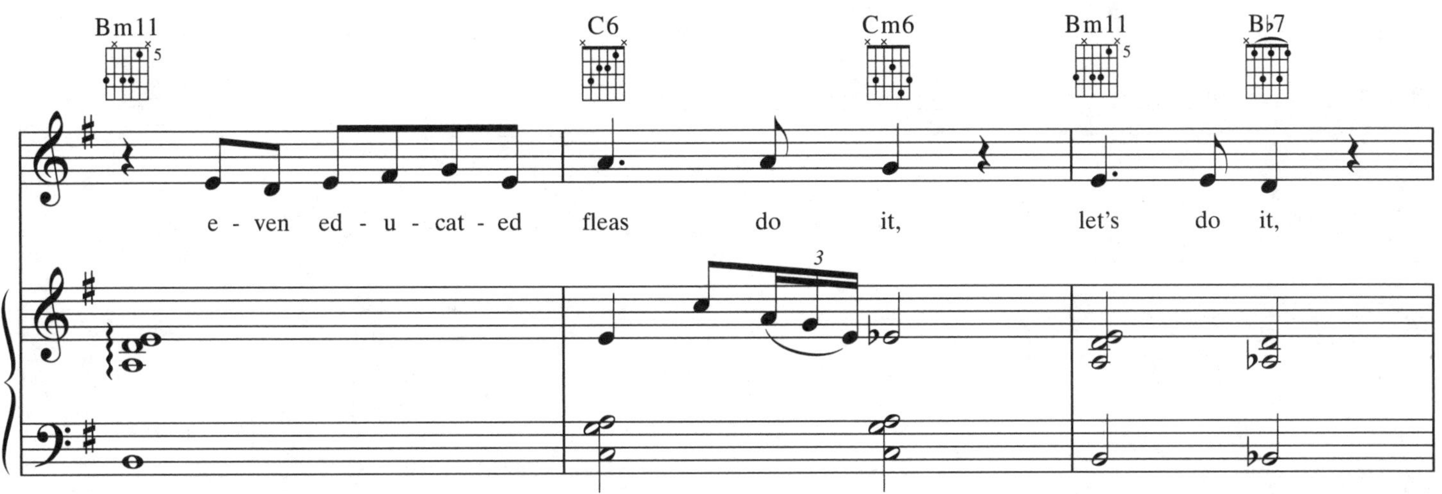

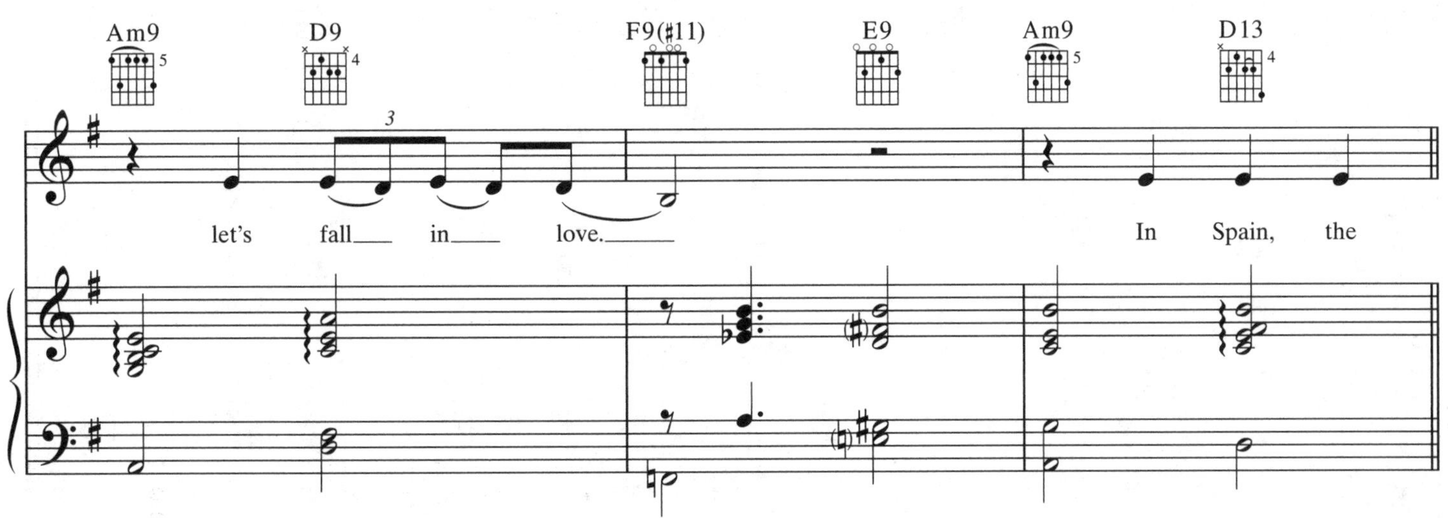

Easy swing (𝅗𝅥 = 69)
G(9) D7 G C6 Cm6
best up - per sets do it, Lith - u - an - i - ans and Letts do it,
mf
Bm7 B♭9 Am7 D7 G C7 G N.C.
let's do it, let's fall in love. The Dutch in
3
Em Am7 Bm7 G7 G13
old Am - ster - dam do it, not to men - tion the Finns.
C F7 B♭ Am11 D9(♯5)
Folks in Si - am do it, think of Si - am - ese twins. Some Ar - gen -

G6
Am7
D7
G
C7
Cm
tines, with-out means, do it, peo-ple say, in Bos-ton, e-ven beans do it,
Bm7
Em7
Am7
D7
G
Cm
G
N.C.
let's do it, let's fall in love.
2. Ro-man-tic
Refrain:
G6
D7
G
C
Cm
spong-es, they say, do it, oys-ters, down in Oys-ter Bay, do it,
Bm7
B♭7
Am7
D7
G
Em7
Am
D9(♯5)
let's do it, let's fall in love.
Cold Cape Cod

G
D7
G
C6
Cm6
clams, 'gainst their wish, do it, e - ven laz - y jel - ly - fish do it,
Bm7
B♭7
Am7
D7
G
Cm
G
N.C.
3
lets' do it, let's fall in love. E - lec - tric
Em
Am9
Bm7
G7
5
eels, I might add, do it, though it shocks 'em I know.
C
F7
B♭
Am11
D9(♯5)
Why ask if shad do it, wait - er, bring me shad roe. In shal - low

G
D7
G
C7
Cm6
shoals, En-glish soles do it, gold-fish, in the pri-va-cy of bowls, do it,
Bm7
Em7
Am7(♭5)
D7
G
Cm
G
N.C.
let's do it, let's fall in love.
3. The dra-gon-
Refrain:
Bm7
E7
A6
A13
D7
Dm6
flies, in the reeds, do it, sen-ti-men-tal cen-ti-pedes do it,
C♯m11
C9
Bm7
E9
A
Dm6
A
E9(♯5)
let's do it, let's fall in love.
Mos-qui-toes,

A6
A+
A
Bm7
E7
A6
D6
Dm
heav - en for - bid, do it, so does ev - 'ry ka - ty - did, do it,
C♯m7
C7
Bm7
E9
A
Dm6
A
N.C.
let's do it, let's fall in love. The most re -
rall.
Slow swing ♩ = 100
F♯m7
Bm7
C♯m7
A9
fined la - dy bugs do it when a gen - tle - man calls.
Dmaj7
G9
C
Bm11
E9(♯5)
Moths in your rugs do it, what's the use of moth balls? Lo - custs in

A6
Bm7
E7(♭9)
A6
trees do it,
bees do it,
e - ven o - ver - ed - u - cat - ed
accel. poco a poco
Tempo segundo (𝅗𝅥 = 69)
D7
Dm
C♯m7
F♯m7
Bm7(♭5)
E7
A
Dm6
fleas do it,
let's do it,
let's fall in love.
C♯m7
F♯m7
Bm7
A/E
E7
A
Dm6
Let's do it,
let's fall in love.
C♯m7
F♯m7
Bm7(♭5)
E7
A
Dm6
A
Let's do it,
let's fall in love.

LOVE IS A MANY SPLENDORED THING

Lyric by
PAUL FRANCIS WEBSTER

Music by
SAMMY FAIN

F7 B♭ F7 B♭
and I said, "Can you tell me, please, where's that love I've nev - er found?
Fm7 B♭7 Fm7
Un - rav - el me this rid - dle: What is love? What can it
B♭7 Fm7/B♭ B♭9 B♭dim Fm7 B♭7sus B♭7
be?" And in her eyes were but - ter - flies as she re - plied to me.
colla voce
poco rit.
Chorus:
E♭ Cm Gm B♭m7/E♭ E♭7
Love is a man - y - splen - dored thing. It's the
mp-mf

A♭
A♭6
A♭maj7
Fm6
Cm
Fm6
Cm
Ap - ril rose that on - ly grows in the ear - ly spring.
Love is
Fm7
Cm7/B♭
Dm7(♭5)/A♭
G7(♭9)
na - ture's way of giv - ing a rea - son to be liv - ing.
The
Cm
Cm7
D7
G
B♭7
gold - en crown that makes a man a king.
E♭
Cm
Gm
B♭m7/E♭
E♭7
Once on a high and wind - y hill,
in the

A♭ A♭maj7 A♭6 A♭ Gm7 C9 Gm7 C7
morn - ing mist, two lov - ers kissed and the world stood still, then your
Fm Fm7 Dm7(♭5) G7(♯5) C7(♯5) C7 F7 A♭m6
fin - gers touched my si - lent heart and taught it how to sing. Yes,
poco rit.
Slower
E♭/B♭ Cm Fm7 A♭/B♭ B♭7(♭9) 1. E♭
true love's a man - y - splen - dored thing.
Fm7 B♭7(♭9) 2. E♭ Fm7 E♭
thing.
rall.

LOVE IS HERE TO STAY

Lyrics by
IRA GERSHWIN

Music by
GEORGE GERSHWIN

Con anima

Gm7 Gm7/C

mp *mf*

C7 F6 Fmaj7 D7 G7

The more I read the pa - pers, the less I com - pre -

mp leggiero

D7 Gm7 Cdim7 C9 F/A A♭dim7

hend the world and all its ca - pers and how it all will

Gm7
C7
B♭
F(9)/A
G7
end. Noth - ing seems to be last - ing, but that is - n't our af -
C7
B♭
Em7(♭5)
A7
D
fair; we've got some - thing per - ma - nent, I mean in the way
G7
C9
we care. It's ver - y
Refrain:
G9
Gm7
C7
F
Gm7
C7
clear our love is here to stay; not for a
p - mf

G7 Gm7 C7 E♭9 D9 G7
year, but ev - er and a day. The ra - di -
C7 D7 Gm7 C7 Fmaj7 B♭ Em7(♭5) A7
o and the tel - e - phone and the mov - ies that we know may just be
Dm G7 Gm7 C7
pass - ing fan - cies, and in time may go. But, oh my
mf
p
G9 Gm7 C7 F Gm7 C7
dear, our love is here to stay. To - geth - er

G7 Gm7 C7 E♭9 D9 G7

we're go - ing a long, long way. In time the

C7 D7 Gm7 C7 E♭9 D7

Rock - ies may crum - ble, Gi - bral - tar may tum - ble. They're on - ly made of

B♭6 Bdim7 F/C Gm7 C9

clay, but our love is here to

8va *mp* *dim.*

1. F6 C7 — 2. F6 C13 Fmaj13

stay.______ It's ver - y stay.______

p *mf* *pp delicato*

Ped. *

MISTY

Lyrics by
JOHNNY BURKE

Music by
ERROLL GARNER

Misty - 3 - 1

Ebmaj7 Bbm7 Eb7-9 Abmaj7
way and a thou-sand vi-o-lins be-gin to play, or it might be the
3 3 3 3
Abm Db9 Ebmaj7 Cm Fm7 Bb7-9
sound of your hel-lo, that mu - sic I hear, I get mist-y, the mo-ment you're
Eb Cm7 Fm7 Bb7-9 Eb6 Ddim Eb6 Bbm7
near. You can say that you're lead-ing me on,
Eb7-9 Abmaj7 Ab6 Bbdim Ab6
but it's just what I want you to do. Don't you no-tice how

Am7
D7
F7
Bb
Edim
Fm7
Bb7-9
Bb9
hope-less-ly I'm lost, that's why I'm fol-low-ing you. On my
Ebmaj7
Bbm7
Eb7-9
Abmaj7
own, would I wan-der through this won-der-land a-lone, nev-er know-ing my
Abm
Db9
Ebmaj7
Cm
Fm7
Bb7-9
right foot from my left, my hat from my glove, I'm too mist-y and too much in
Eb
E9
Fm7
Bb7+
Bb9
Eb
Abmaj7
Gm7
E7
Ebmaj7
1.
2.
love. Look at love.
mf

MY FUNNY VALENTINE

Words by
LORENZ HART

Music by
RICHARD RODGERS

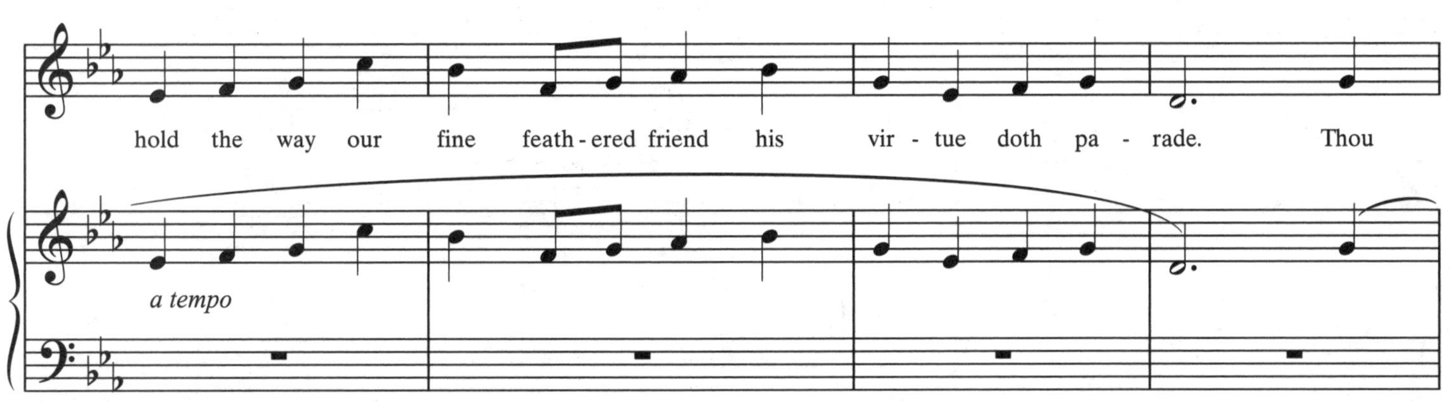

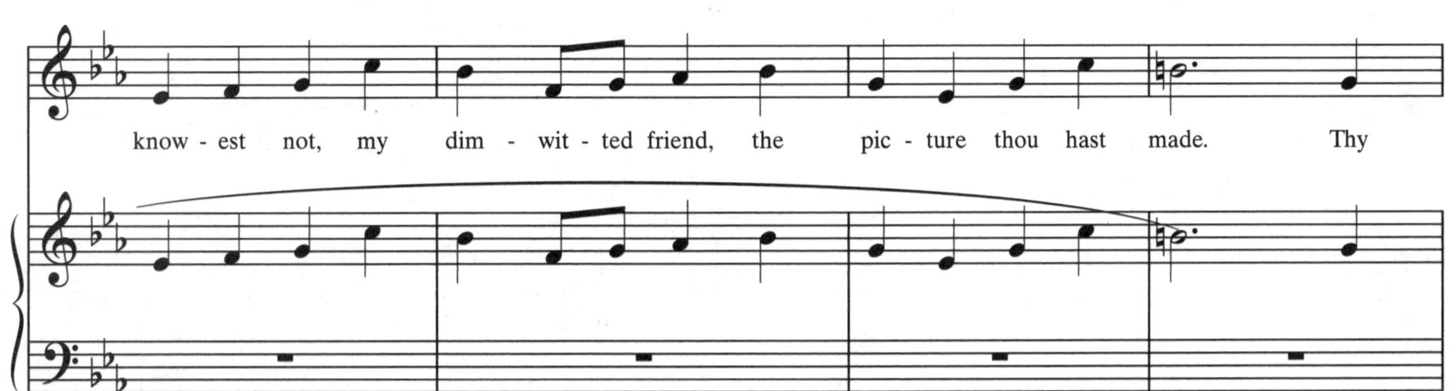

va - cant brow and thy tou - sled hair con - ceal thy good in - tent. Thou
no - ble, up - right, truth - ful, sin - cere, and slight - ly dop - ey gent. You're
G7(♯5)
rall.
p
Slowly, in tempo
Refrain:
Cm
Cm(maj7)
Cm7
Cm6
my fun - ny val - en - tine, sweet com - ic val - en - tine,
A♭
Fm7
Dm7(♭5)
G7
Dm7(♭5)
G7
you make me smile with my heart.

Cm
Cm(maj7)
Cm7
Cm6
Your looks are laugh - a - ble, un - pho - to - graph - a - ble,
A♭
Fm7
Fm7(♭5)
B♭7
Yet, you're my fa - v'rite work of art. Is your
E♭
Fm7
B♭7
fig - ure less than Greek? Is your mouth a lit - tle weak? When you
mf
E♭maj7
G7
Cm
A♭
A♭7
G9
o - pen it to speak, are you smart? But

128
Cm
Cm(maj7)
Cm7
don't change a hair for me, not if you
mp
Cm6
A♭
D7(♭5)
G7
care for me. Stay, lit - tle val - en - tine,
poco a poco cresc.
Cm
E♭7
A♭
A♭/G
Fm7
B♭9
stay!
Each day is Val - en - tine's
f
mf
1. E♭
A♭7
G7
2. E♭
Day.
Day.
mf
p
8vb
My Funny Valentine - 4 - 4

NEVER MY LOVE

Words and Music by
DON and DICK ADDRISI

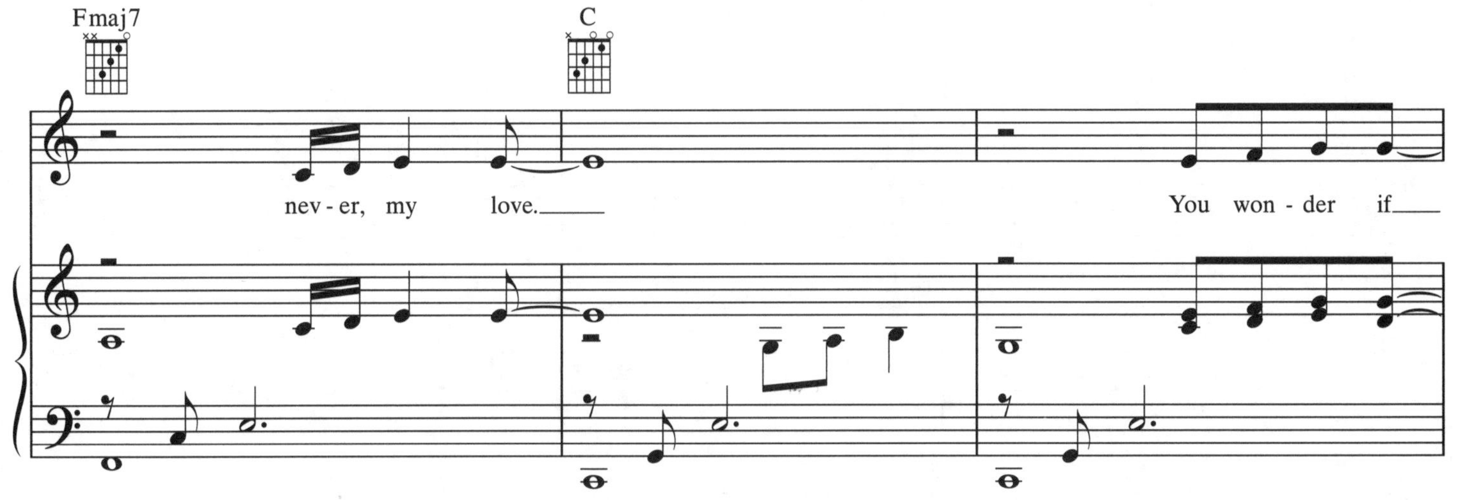

Never My Love - 3 - 1

G/B
B♭
F/A
C/G
this heart of mine will lose its de - sire for you.
Am
C
Fmaj7
Nev - er, my love,
nev - er, my love.
C
E7sus
E7
Am7
D9
1. What makes you think love will end, when you
2. How can you think love will end, when I've
mf
Gmaj7
Cmaj9
Fmaj7
Dm7
know that my whole life de - pends on
asked you to spend your whole life with

Em7
To Coda
Am
C
you?
me?
You say you fear
rit.
a tempo
mp
G/B
B♭
F/A
C/G
I'll change my mind,
I won't re - quire
you.
Am
C
Fmaj7
C
D.S. al Coda
Nev-er, my love,
nev-er, my love.
Coda
Am9
decresc.
8va
ppp

From the United Artists Motion Picture "THE SPY WHO LOVED ME"

NOBODY DOES IT BETTER

Lyrics by
CAROLE BAYER SAGER

Music by
MARVIN HAMLISCH

Gm7
Gm7/C
C7
F
F7
Fdim7
B♭m
E
Ba - by, you're the best.
Did you have to be so good?
F
F7/A
B♭
B♭m
I was - n't look - in'
but some-how you found me.
The way that you hold me
when - ev - er you hold me.
F
F7/A
G9
G♭9
I tried to hide from your love - light,
There's some kind of mag - ic in - side you

F
F7/A
B♭
B♭m
but like heav-en a-bove_ me,___ the spy who loved_ me___ is
that keeps me from run - nin'.___ But just keep it com - in',___
A7
D7(♭9)
Gm7
C7
1.
F
keep - in' all my se - crets safe to - night.
how'd you learn to do the things you
2.
F
B♭
B♭m
do? And No - bod - y does__ it

F7
B♭
B♭m
F7
bet - ter,
makes me feel sad
for the
rest.

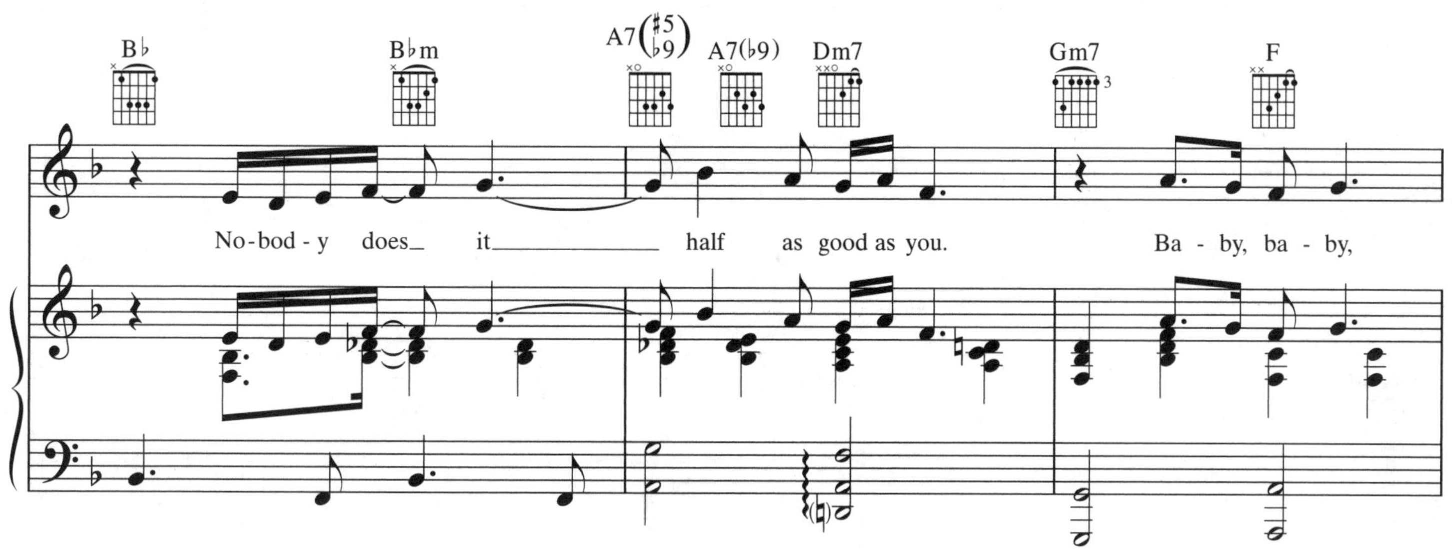
B♭
B♭m
A7(♯5 ♭9)
A7(♭9)
Dm7
Gm7
F
No-bod - y does
it
half
as good as you.
Ba - by, ba - by,

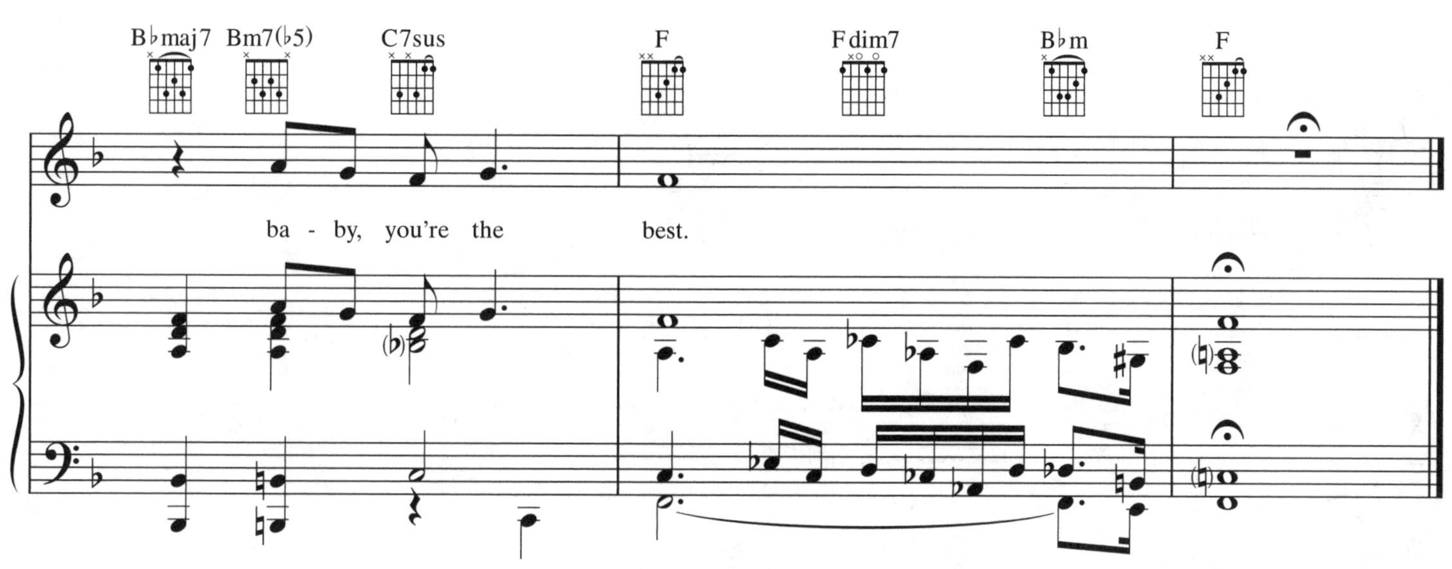
B♭maj7
Bm7(♭5)
C7sus
F
Fdim7
B♭m
F
ba - by, you're the
best.

RIGHT HERE WAITING

Words and Music by
RICHARD MARX

Csus2/F
Dm7add4
3fr.
G/B
Am
on the line, but it doesn't stop the pain. If I see you next
ter, I taste the tears, but I can't get near you now. Oh, can't you see
Fsus2/D
Am
Fsus2/D
Fsus2/G
to nev - er, how can we say for - ev - er.
it, ba - by, you've got me go - in' cra - zy.
C
G
Am
Wher - ev - er you go, what - ev - er you do, I will be right
F
G
C
G
here wait - ing for you. What - ev - er it takes, or how my heart breaks,
Am
F
G
To Coda
1.
Am
I will be right here wait - ing for you.

2.
Fsus2/D
C/E
Fadd2
I won - der how we can sur - vive this ro - mance.
Fsus2/D
C/E
But in the end if I'm with you,
Fadd2
Gsus4
G/B
C
I'll take the chance.
G
Am
F
G
C

G
Am
F
G
Am
D.S. (lyric 2) al Coda
Oh, can't you see
Coda
C
G
Am
F
G
C
G
Wait - ing for you.
Am
F
Gsus4
G
C
rit.

THE ROSE

Words and Music by
AMANDA McBROOM

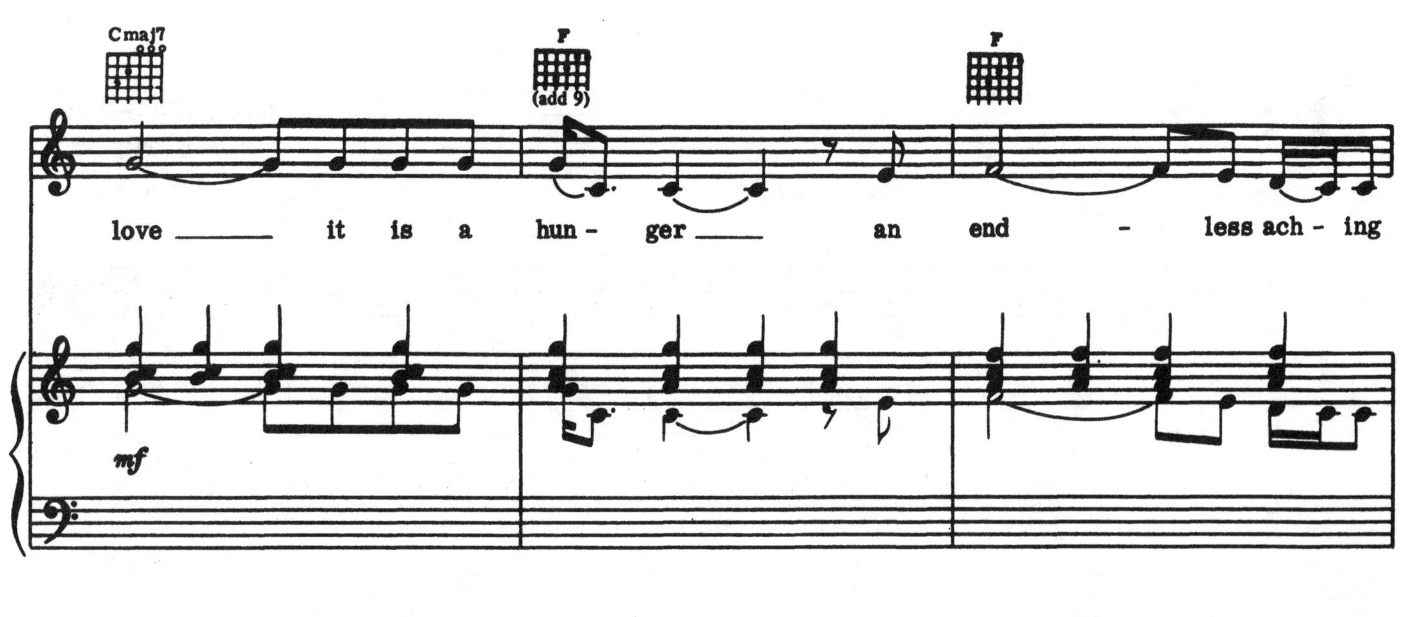
Cmaj7
F
(add 9)
F
love it is a hun- ger an end - less ach - ing
mf

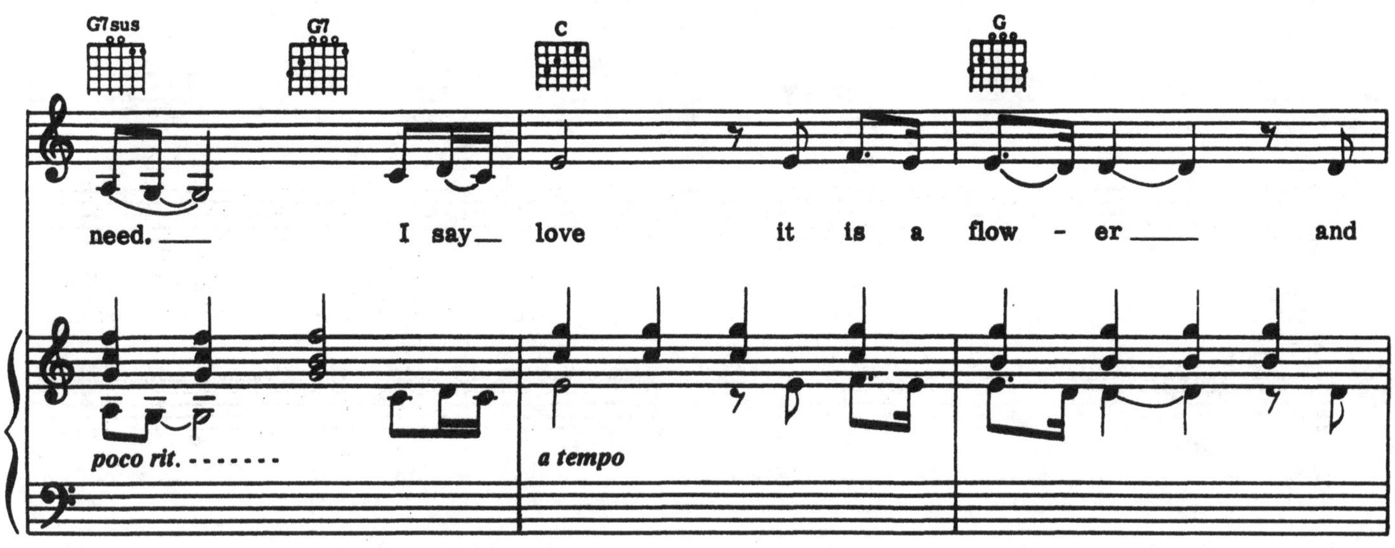
G7sus
G7
C
G
need. I say love it is a flow - er and
poco rit.
a tempo

F
C
you it's on - ly seed. It's the
poco cresc.

G
F
G
heart a - fraid of break - ing that nev - er learns to
night has been too lone - ly and the road has been too
mf-f
C
G
dance. It's the dream a - fraid of wak - ing that
long, and you think that love is on - ly for the
F
G
C
Em
(B Bass)
Em
nev - er takes the chance. It's the one who won't
luck - y and the strong, just re - mem - ber in the
f
Am7
Am7
(G Bass)
F
G
be tak - en who can - not seem to give, and the
win - ter far be - neath the bit - ter snows lies the
rit.
mf

C
G
1. F
G
soul a - fraid of dy - in' that never learns to
seed that with the sun's love in the
a tempo
cresc.
C
live.
When the
f
2. F
G
C
spring be - comes the rose.
mf
rit.
a tempo
play 3 times
rit. . . . .

SAVE THE LAST DANCE FOR ME

Words by
DOC POMUS

Music by
MORT SHUMAN

E♭ B♭7 E♭7 A♭

pale moon - light. }
an - y - one. }
But don't for - get who's tak - ing you

E♭

home and in whose arms you're go - na be.
So,

B♭7 1. E♭

dar - lin', save the last dance for me.
2. Oh, I

2. E♭ N.C. *Bridge:* B♭7

me.
Ba - by, don't you know I love you so?

E♭
N.C.
Can't you feel it when we touch?
I will nev - er, nev - er
B♭7
E♭
let you go.
I love you, oh, so much.
Verse:
You can dance, go and car - ry on till the
B♭7
night is gone and it's time to go.
If he

asks if you're all a - lone, can he take you home, you must
Eb
Bb7
Eb7
Ab
tell him no. 'Cause don't for - get who's tak - ing you
Eb
home and in whose arms you're go - na be. So,
Bb7
Eb
dar - lin', save the last dance for me.

METRO-GOLDWYN-MAYER presents DAVID LEAN'S FILM "DOCTOR ZHIVAGO"

SOMEWHERE, MY LOVE

(Lara's Theme From "Doctor Zhivago")

Lyric by
PAUL FRANCIS WEBSTER

Music by
MAURICE JARRE

Moderately, with expression
Refrain:
G
B♭dim7
D7
Some - where, my love, there will be songs to sing,
p-mf
Am7
D7
Am7
D7
G
al - though the snow cov - ers the hope of spring.
B♭dim7
D7
Some - where a hill blos-soms in green and gold,

Am7 D7 Am7 D7 G
and there are dreams, all that your heart can hold.
C G
Some - day we'll meet a - gain, my love.
B♭ F B♭ D7
Some - day when-ev-er the spring breaks through.
G B♭dim7 D7
You'll come to me out of the long a - go.

Am7
D7
G
Warm as the wind,
soft as the kiss of snow.
B♭dim7
Till then, my sweet,
(Lau - ra, my own,)
think of me now and then.
1.
God - speed, my love,
till you are mine a - gain.
2.
D7(♭9)
till you are mine a - gain.
rit. e dim.

TAKE MY BREATH AWAY

Words by
TOM WHITLOCK

Music by
GIORGIO MORODER

G
D/F♯
Em7
on this end-less o - cean, fi - n'lly lov-ers know no shame.
Nev-er hes - i - tat - ing to be-come the fat - ed ones.
D/F♯
Am
G
Turn-ing and re - turn - ing to some se - cret place in - side,
D/F♯
G
watch-ing in slow mo - tion as
D/F♯
C(9)/E
D/F♯
you turn a-round and say, my love, "Take my breath a -

Chorus:
G
D/F♯
C(9)/E
way.
D/F♯
G
D/F♯
Take my breath a - way."
1.
2.
C(9)/E
D/F♯
D/F♯
Bridge:
Am
D
C(9)
Through the ho - ur - glass I saw you. In time, you slipped a - way.

G
Am
D
When the mir - ror crashed, I called you and turned
C(9)
G
A(9)
to hear you say, "If on - ly for to - day,
D
N.C.
I am un - a - fraid."
Take my breath a -
B♭
F/A
E♭(9)/G
F
Repeat ad lib. and fade
way.
Take my breath a -

THEME FROM "ICE CASTLES" (THROUGH THE EYES OF LOVE)

Lyrics by
CAROLE BAYER SAGER

Music by
MARVIN HAMLISCH

Cm7
Cm7
(F Bass)
F9
(Eb Bass)
Dm7
Gm7
Dm7
Cm7
Cm7
(F Bass)
F7
(Eb Bass)
Dm7
Gm7
I can see what's mine now finding out what's true
Reach-ing out to touch you I can feel so much
how it feels to touch you, how I feel so much
since
cresc.
Ebmaj7
Eb6
D7sus
D7
Gm7
Gm7
(F Bass)
C9
(E Bass)
To Coda
1.
Cm7
I found you look-ing through the eyes of
f
mf
Cm7
(F Bass)
2.
Cm7
Cm7
(F Bass)
Bb
love. 2. And through the eyes of love. And

Gm
Dm7
Gm
Dm7
Cm7
Cm7
(F Bass)
now I do be - lieve that e - ven in the storm we'll find some
f
Bb
Cm7
Dm7
Eb
Bb
(D Bass)
C7
Cm7
(F Bass)
light. Know - ing you're be - side me I'm all right.
mf
cresc.
f
mf
D.S. al Coda
Coda
Cm7
Cm7
(F Bass)
Bb
through the eyes of love.
mf
rit.

THIS I PROMISE YOU

Words and Music by
RICHARD MARX

Asus
A
A2
Bm7
fore.
and all that sur - rounds you
And I prom-ise you, nev - er
G(9)
Asus
A
Em7
are se - crets and lies,
will you hurt an - y - more.
I'll be your strength,
I give you my word. I
A7
D
A/C♯
Bm7
I'll give you hope,
give you my heart.
keep-ing your faith when it's gone.
This is a bat - tle we've won.
The
And
omit 2nd time
Em7
Gm6
Asus
one you should call
with this vow,
was stand-ing here all a - long.
for - ev - er has now be - gun.
3

Chorus:
Asus
A
D
A
And I will take you in my arms and
Just close your eyes each lov-ing day and
3. (Inst. solo ad lib....
Bm7
G
D/A
To Coda
hold you right where you be-long.
know this feel-ing won't go a-way.
'Til the day my life is
A
Gmaj9
1.
D
through, this I prom-ise you.
This I prom-ise you.
2.
D
Bridge:
Em7
A
ise you.
O-ver and o-ver I fall

Em7
A
D
A
G
when I hear you call. With-out you in my life,
D.S. 𝄋 al Coda
Em7
Asus
A
baby, I just would-n't be liv - ing at all.
𝄌 Coda
Chorus:
A
N.C.
E
B
…end solo) And I will take you in my arms and
close your eyes each lov - ing day and
C♯m7
A
E/B
hold you right where you be - long. 'Til the day my life is
know this feel - ing won't go a - way. Ev - 'ry word I say is

1.
B
A
2.
B
through, this I prom - ise you. Just through, this I prom -
Amaj9
E
ise you. Ev - 'ry word I say is
B
Amaj9
true, this I prom - ise you. Ooh, I prom -
E
A/E
E
A/E
E
ise you.
rit.

THIS KISS

Words and Music by
ROBIN LERNER, ANNIE ROBOFF
and BETH NIELSEN CHAPMAN

B G♯m7 A F♯m7

But you got me like a rock - et shoot-ing straight a - cross__ the sky.
Ride me off in - to the sun - set, ba - by, I'm for - ev - er yours.

Chorus:

E E/G♯ A B

It's the way__ you love me. It's a feel - ing like this.__

E E/G♯ A B

It's cen - trif - u - gal mo - tion. It's per - pet - u - al bliss.__

E E/G♯ A B

It's that piv - ot - al mo - ment. It's, *ah,*__ {im - pos - si - ble. / un - think - a - ble.}

E E/G♯ A C♯m7 B

This kiss,__ this kiss,__ {un - stop - a - ble. / un - sink - a - ble.}

1.
2.
E
E/G♯
A
C♯m7
B
This kiss, this kiss.
Bridge:
C
Am7
D/F♯
G
You can kiss me in the moon-light, on the roof-top, un-der the sky, oh.
You can kiss me with the win-dows o-pen while the rain comes blow-in' in-side, oh.
C/B
Kiss me in sweet, slow mo-tion. Let's let ev-'ry-thing slide.
F♯m7
F♯m7/B
You got me float-ing, you got me fly-ing.

F♯ F♯/A♯ B C♯

It's the way you love me. It's a feel-ing like this.

F♯ F♯/A♯ B C♯ F♯ F♯/A♯

It's cen-trif-u-gal mo-tion. It's per-pet-u-al bliss. It's that piv-ot-al mo-ment.

B C♯ F♯ F♯/A♯ B D♯m7 C♯

It's, *ah,* sub-lim-i-nal. This kiss, this kiss. It's crim-i-nal.

F♯ F♯/A♯ B D♯m7 C♯ F♯ F♯/A♯

This kiss, this kiss. It's the way you love me,

Repeat and fade

B D♯m7 C♯ F♯ F♯/A♯ B D♯m7 C♯

ba - by. It's the way you love me, dar - ling.

THIS MAGIC MOMENT

Words and Music by
DOC POMUS and MORT SHUMAN

Gm
took me by sur - prise. I knew that you felt it, too
Eb
By the
F7
look in your eyes,
no chord
Sweet - er than
Gm
wine,
Soft - er than a
Eb
sum - mer night.
Ev - 'ry - thing I want I have
Bb
When - ev - er I
F7
hold you tight.
no chord
This mag - ic
Bb
mo - ment,
while your

Gm
Eb
lips are close to mine, Will last for - ev - er,
For -
F7
Bb
ev - er, till the end of time.
Oh.
Gm
Eb
1. F7
Oh.
Oh.
no chord
This mag - ic
2. F7
Bb
Oh.

TRUE LOVE

(from "High Society")

Words and Music by
COLE PORTER

Ab
Abm6
Eb/Bb
F9
Fm7
Bb7
far a-bove par; oh, how luck-y we are. While I
Refrain:
Eb
Ab
Ebdim7
Eb
Bb7
give to you and you give to me true
love, true love. So, on and on it will
Ebdim7
Eb
Bb7
al-ways be true love, true

E♭ A♭m7 D♭7 G♭ E♭9
love. For you and I have a guard - ian an - gel on
A♭m7 D♭7 G♭ B♭7 E♭
high with noth - ing to do but to give to
rit.
a tempo
A♭ E♭dim7 E♭ B♭7
1.
you and you give to me love for - ev - er -
E♭ Fm B♭
2.
B♭7 E♭
more. I love for - ev - er - more.
rit.

WAY BACK INTO LOVE
(from "Music and Lyrics")
Words and Music by
ADAM SCHLESINGER
Moderately ♩ = 104
Guitar Capo 1 →
Piano →
A F♯m A F♯m
B♭ Gm B♭ Gm
mp
Bm7 Esus E Bm7 Esus E
Cm7 Fsus F Cm7 Fsus F
Verses 1 & 2:
A F♯m7 A
B♭ Gm7 B♭
Female: 1. I've been liv-ing with a shad-ow o-ver head. I've been sleep-ing with a
Male: 2. I've been hid-ing all my hopes and dreams a-way, just in case I ev-er
mf a tempo
F♯m7 Bm7(4) Esus E
Gm7 Cm7(4) Fsus F
cloud a-bove my bed. I've been lone-ly for so long,
need 'em a-gain some day. I've been set-ting a-side time to
Way Back Into Love - 7 - 1

1.
2.
Bm7(4)
Esus
E
E2
E
Esus
E
E2
E
Cm7(4)
Fsus
F
F2
F
Fsus
F
F2
F
trapped in the past, I just can't seem to move on. ners of my mind.
clear a lit - tle space in the cor -
Chorus:
A
F♯m7
D(9)
B♭
Both:
Gm7
E♭(9)
All I wan-na do is find a way back in - to love.
A
F♯m7
B♭
Gm7
I can't make it through with - out a way
D(9)
A
E7sus
E
E♭(9)
B♭
F7sus
F
back in - to love.
Oh.

Verses 3 & 4:
D/E
E
A
F♯m7(4)
E♭/F
F
B♭
Gm7(4)
F: 3. I've been watch-ing, but the stars re-fuse to shine.
M: 4. I've been look-ing for some-one to shed some light,
A
F♯m7(4)
Bm7(4)
B♭
Gm7(4)
Cm7(4)
I've been search-ing, but I just don't see the signs. I know that it's out
not some-bod-y just to get me through the night. I could use some di-rec-
Esus
E
Bm7(4)
Fsus
F
Cm7(4)
1.
Esus
E
E2
E
Fsus
F
F2
F
there. There's got-ta be some-thing for my soul, some-where.
tion, and I'm o-pen to your
2. Esus
E
E2
E
Fsus
F
F2
F
Chorus:
A
F♯m7(4)
B♭
Gm7(4)
Both:
sug-ges-tions. All I wan-na do is find a way

D(9)
A
E♭(9)
B♭
back in - to love.
I can't make it
F♯m7(4)
D(9)
A
Gm7(4)
E♭(9)
B♭
through with - out a way back in - to love.
And if I
And if I
E7
F7
To Coda
o - pen my heart a - gain,
o - pen my heart to you,
I guess I'm
I'm hop - ing
hop - ing you'll be there for
A
F♯m7(4)
B♭
Gm7(4)
F:
me in the end.
Oh.

A
B♭
F♯m7(4)
Gm7(4)
M:
Bm7(4)
Cm7(4)
Oh, oh.
Esus
Fsus
E
F
F:
Bm7(4)
Cm7(4)
Oh.
Esus E E2 E
Fsus F F2 F
Verse 5:
A
B♭
F:
F♯m7(4)
Gm7(4)
A
B♭
5. There are mo-ments when I don't know if it's real, or if an-y-bod-y
F♯m7(4)
Gm7(4)
Bm7
Cm7
Esus
Fsus
E
F
feels the way I feel. I need in-spi-ra-tion,

D.S. 𝄋 al Coda
Bm7
Cm7
Esus
Fsus
E
F
not just an - oth - er ne - go - ti - a - tion.
𝄌 Coda
F♯m7(4)
Gm7(4)
Bm7
Cm7
you'll show me what to do. And if you help me to start a - gain,
E7sus
F7sus
E
F
D/E
E♭/F
E
F
you know that I'll be there for you in the end.
A
B♭
F♯m7(4)
Gm7(4)
A
B♭
F: Oh.

F♯m7(4)
Gm7(4)
Bm7(4)
Cm7(4)
Esus
Fsus
E
F
F: Oh.
M: Whoa.
F: Oh, oh.
M: Oh, oh.
Bm7(4)
Cm7(4)
1.
Esus
Fsus
E
F
E2
F2
E
F
2.
Esus
Fsus
E
F
E2
F2
E
F
A
B♭
M: Oh, oh.
F: Oh.
mp
F♯m
Gm
A
B♭
F♯m
Gm
A
B♭
rit.

WEDDING SONG
(There Is Love)

Moderately, flowing

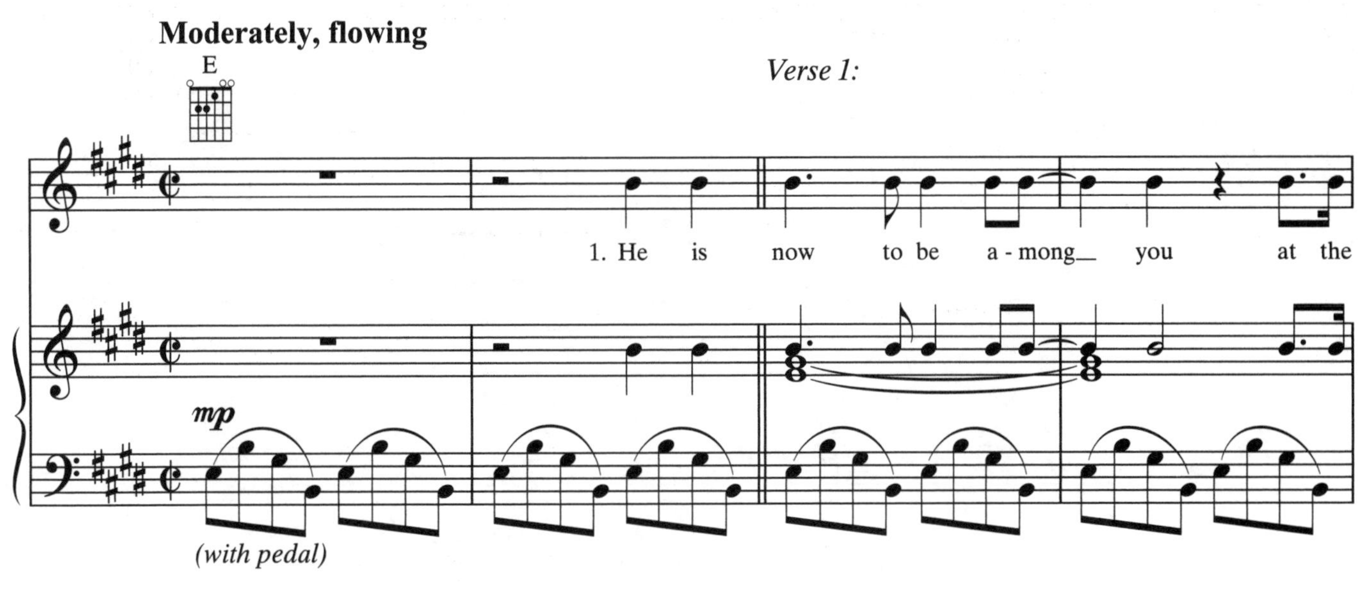

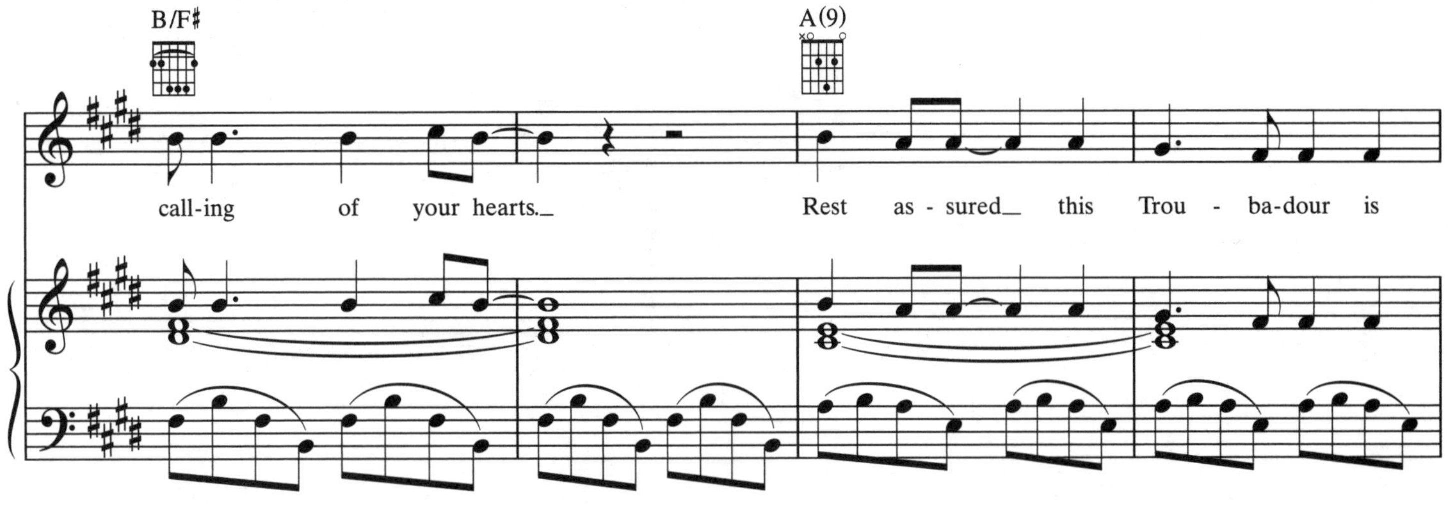

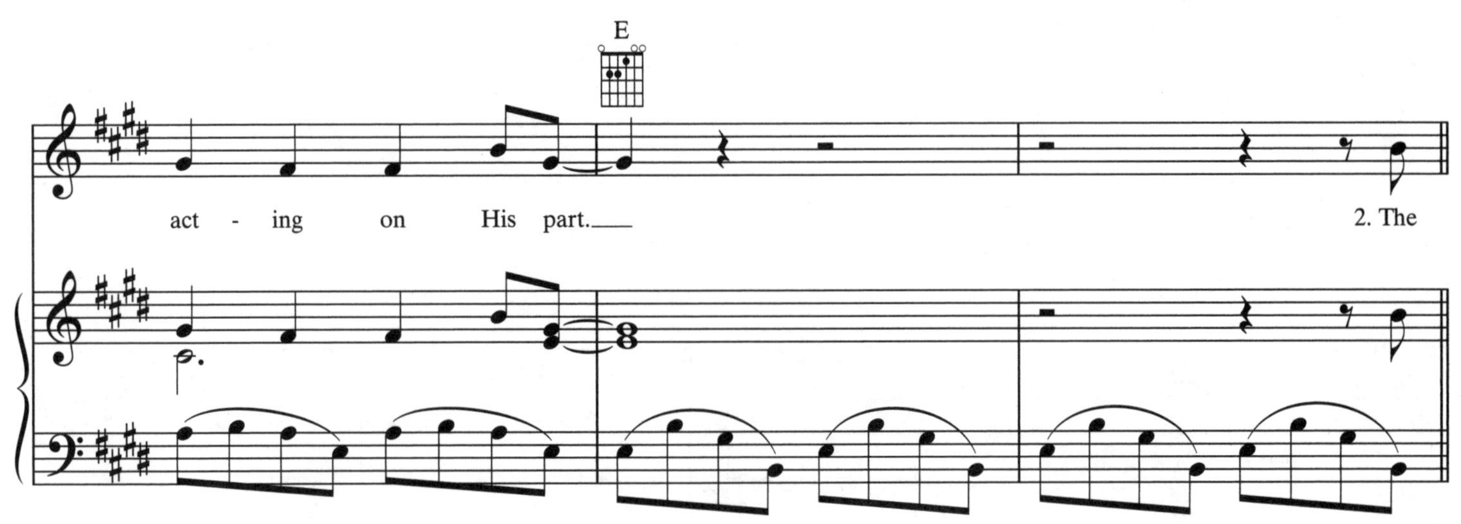

Verses 2, 3, & 4:
E
B/F♯
A(9)
E
un - ion of your spir - its here has caused Him to re - main, for when -
(3.) was in the be - gin - ning is now and till the end,
(4.) mar - riage of your spir - its here has caused Him to re - main, for when -
C♯m
E
B/F♯
ev - er two or more of you are gath - ered in his name, there is
wom - an draws her life from man and gives it back a - gain, and there is
ev - er two or more of you are gath - ered in his name, there is
A
love, there is
love, there is
love, oh, there's
E
F♯7/E
To Coda
love.
love.
love.

A(9)
E
1.
3. Well, a
Verse 3:
B/F♯
A(9)
man shall leave his moth-er, and a wom-an leave her home.
E
C♯m
E
They shall trav-el on to where the
B/F♯
2.
two shall be as one. As it
Well, then

Bridge:
A
A/G♯
F♯m
B
E
what's to be the rea - son for be - com-ing man and wife? Is it
A
A/G♯
F♯m
B
love that brings you here or love that brings you life?
E
B/F♯
For if lov - ing is the an - swer, then
A(9)
E
C♯m
who's the giv - ing for? Do you be - lieve in

E
B/F♯
some - thing that you've nev - er seen__ be - fore?__ Oh, there's
A(9)
love,__ oh, there's
E
D.S. 𝄋 al Coda
love.__ 4. Oh, the
𝄌 Coda
A(9)
E
rit.

WHAT ARE YOU DOING THE REST OF YOUR LIFE?

Lyrics by
ALAN and MARILYN BERGMAN

Music by
MICHEL LEGRAND

Am (G bass)
Am (F# bass)
Fmaj7
All the nick-els and the dimes of your days. Let the rea-sons and the
Dm7
Bm7-5
E7
Amaj7
A
rhymes of your days all be-gin and end with me. I want to
Bm7-5
E9
Amaj7
Bm7-5
E9
see your face in ev-'ry kind of light. In fields of dawn and for-ests of the
Amaj7
Abm7
Db7-9
Gbmaj7
night. And when you stand be-fore the can-dles on a cake, Oh, let me be the
Gm7
C7-9
Fmaj9
Am
Am (G# bass)
one to hear the si-lent wish you make! Those to-mor-rows wait-ing deep in your eyes,

Am (G bass)
Am (F♯ bass)
Fmaj7
In the world of love you keep in your eyes, I'll a - wak - en what's a -
Dm7
Bm7-5
Bm7 (E bass)
E7
sleep in your eyes. It may take a kiss or two! Thru
cresc.
F6
Bm7-5
E9
Fmaj7
all of my life, Sum - mer, win - ter, spring and fall of my life,
F7-5
Am (E bass)
Bm7
E7+5
E7
All I ev - er will re - call of my life is all of my life with
1 Am
Bm7-5
E7
you! What Are You Do - ing The
decresc.
2. Am
Ddim
Am
Ddim
Am
you!
rit. e dim.

WHEN A MAN LOVES A WOMAN

Words and Music by
CALVIN LEWIS and ANDREW WRIGHT

Ab/C
Bbm7
Db/Ab
4fr.
Gb
1.Gb/Ab
see it. She can do_ no wrong._ Turn his back on his best friend if he
com - forts, and sleep out in the rain,__ if she said that's the
3
Db
Gb/Ab
2.Gb/Ab
Db9
puts her down._ When a way_ it ought to be. When a
man loves_ a wom-an,__ I give you ev - ery-thing I've got.__
Try - ing to hold on_ to your pre - cious love._ Ba - by, ba - by,
Eb

Eb7
Ebm7/Ab
11fr.
N.C.
D
please don't treat me bad.
When a man loves a
A/C♯
Bm7
D/A
G
wom - an, deep down in his soul, she can
G/A
3fr.
D
G/A
3fr.
D
bring him such mis - e - ry. If she is play - ing him for a
A/C♯
Bm7
D/A
G
fool, he's the last one to know. Lov - ing

G/A
D
G/A
D
3fr.
eyes can nev - er see.
Yes, when a man loves a
A/C♯
Bm7
D/A
G
freely
wom-an,
I know ex - act - ly how he feels,
'cause
G/A
ba - by,
ba - by...
When a
Repeat and fade
D
A/C♯
Bm7
G/A
man loves a wom - an.
When a

WHEN I FALL IN LOVE

Words by
EDWARD HEYMAN

Music by
VICTOR YOUNG

Ebmaj7 Bbm7 Eb9 Ab Cm7 F9 Bb11 Bb13
know that I'll be true. My first love will be my last.
Chorus:
Eb C7(#5) C7 Fm7 Bb7(b9) Eb
When I fall in love, it will be for - ev - er, or I'll nev - er
C7(#5) C7 Fm7 Bb9 Bb13(b9) Eb/G Bb7(b9)
fall in love. In a rest - less world like this is, love is
Eb/G Db6 C9 Fm7 C7(b9)
end - ed be - fore it's be - gun, and too man - y moon - light kiss - es seem to

Fm
Fm7
B♭11
B♭13(♭9)
E♭
cool in the warmth of the sun.
When I give my heart,
C7(♯5)
Fm7
B♭7(♭9)
E♭
C7(♯5)
Fm7
B♭9
B♭13(♭9)
it will be com - plete - ly,
or I'll nev - er give my heart.
And the
E♭/G
A♭
C7(♯5)
C7
C7(♯5)
Fm
A♭m6
E♭
C7(♭9)
mo - ment I can feel that you feel that way, too,
is when I fall in
Fm7
B♭9
B♭7(♭9)
1.
E♭6
C13
Fm7
B♭7(♭9)
2.
E♭6
Fm7
B♭7(♭9)
E♭maj9
love with you.
you.
rit.

THE WIND BENEATH MY WINGS

Words and Music by
LARRY HENLEY and JEFF SILBAR

Eb(add F)
Bb/D
Cm7
3fr.
face.
You were con -
tent to let me shine,
Fsus4
F
that's your way,
Cm7
3fr.
you al - ways walked a step be - hind.
Fsus4
F
Bb
Eb/Bb
Bb
So, I was the one with all the
It might have ap - peared to go un -

Eb(add F)
Bb
glo - ry,
no - ticed,
while you were the
but I've got it
Eb/Bb
Bb
Eb(add F)
Gm7
3fr.
one with all the strength.
all here in my heart.
Cm7
3fr.
Bb/C
Fsus4
A beau - ti - ful face with - out a name
I want you to know I know the truth, of
F
Cm7
3fr.
Bb/C
Cm7
3fr.
for so long,
course I know it,
a beau - ti - ful smile to hide the
I would be noth - ing with - out

Fsus4
F
D7/F♯
Gm7
3fr.
pain.
you.
Did you ev - er know
F/E♭
E♭
B♭
F/A
that you're my he - ro,
Gm7
3fr.
F/E♭
E♭
B♭
and ev - 'ry - thing I would like to be?
F/A
F
D/F♯
Gm7
3fr.
F/E♭
E♭
I can fly high - er than an

Bb
F/A
Gm7
3fr.
Cm7
3fr.
To Coda
3
ea - gle,
'cause you are the
Fsus4
F
1.
Bb(add C)
3fr.
wind be - neath my wings.
Eb(add F)
3fr.
D.S. al Coda
2.
Bb
Eb/Bb
Bb
F/A
wings.
Coda
Bb/F
F
Bb(add C)
3fr.
wind be - neath my wings.

E♭(add F)/B♭
B♭sus2
F7sus4/E♭
Fly,
fly,
B♭(add C)
3fr.
B♭/D
fly a - way, you let
F7sus4/E♭
F/A
B♭sus2
me fly so high. Oh, fly,

F7sus4/B♭
fly, so
B♭(add C)
3fr.
B♭/D
F7sus4/E♭
high a - gainst the sky, so high I al - most touch
F/A
B♭(add C)
3fr.
the sky. Thank you, thank you, thank
E♭/B♭
Fsus4
B♭(add C)
3fr.
God for you, the wind be - neath my wings.

WOMAN IN LOVE

Words and Music by
BARRY GIBB and ROBIN GIBB

Moderately Slow

Dm C Em7 Am7 B7
I kiss the morn-ing good-bye, but down in - side you know we nev-er know why.
We planned it all at the start, that you and I live in each oth-ers heart.
Em Am Em Am Cmaj7 D7 G
The road is nar-row and long when eyes meet eyes and the feel-ing is strong.
We may be o-ceans a-way you fed my love I hear what you say.
Dm G C G C B7
I turn a-way from the wall. I stum-ble and fall, but I give you it all.
The truth is ev-er a lie. I stum-ble and fall, but I give you it all.
Em B Em B Em B
I am a Wom-an In Love and I'd do an-y-thing to get you in-to my world,

Em
B
Em
D
Am
and hold you with-in
It's a
right
I de- fend
o-ver and o-ver a-
G
Em
To Coda
Cmaj7
D.S. al Coda
gain.
What do I do?
CODA
Em
C9
What do I do?
Fm
C
Fm
C
Fm
C
I am a Wom-an In Love
and I'm talk-ing to you.
I know how you feel,

Fm
C
Fm
Eb
Bbm
what a wom-an can do. It's a right I de - fend
C7
o - ver and o - ver a - gain.
Fm
C
I am a Wom - an In Love,
and I'd do an - y - thing to get you in - to my world, and hold you with - in.
Repeat and Fade
It's a right I de - fend o - ver and o - ver a - gain.

YOU LIGHT UP MY LIFE

Words and Music by
JOE BROOKS

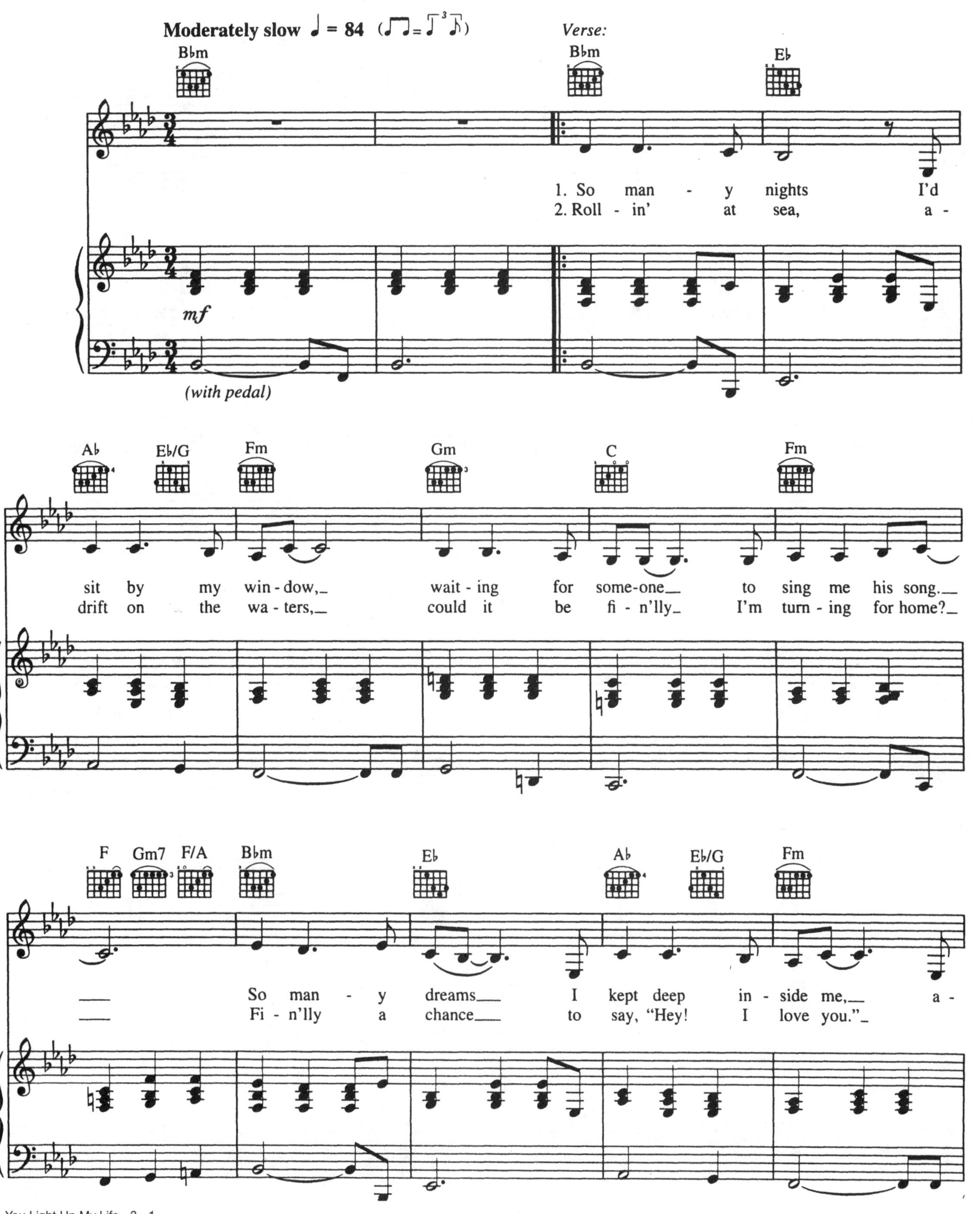

G
B♭
Cm7
B♭/D
lone in the dark, now you've come a - long.
Nev - er a - gain to be all a - lone.
And
E♭
E♭maj7
E♭7
C7
you light up my life. You give me hope
Fm
Fm7
B♭7
To Coda
to car - ry on. You light up my days and fill my
1.
E♭
B♭/D
Cm7
Fm
Fm7
B♭
nights with song.

D.S. 𝄋 al Coda
2.
Eb Bb/D Cm7 Fm Fm7 Bb Cm7 Bb/D
nights with song. 'Cause
⊕ Coda
G7 G7/B Cm F7 Eb/Bb
nights with song. It can't be wrong when
G7/B Cm7 F9 Eb/Bb Bb7sus
it feels so right, 'cause you,
Bb7 Ab Eb Bb7 Ab(9) Eb/G Fm7 Eb
you light up my life.
rit.
a little slower

YOU MAKE ME FEEL SO YOUNG

Words by
JACK GORDON

Music by
JOSEF MYROW

B♭ B♭m B♭dim Gm7 C9 F7
do the cause of it all is you.
B♭ Fdim Cm7 F7 B♭ Fdim
You make me feel so young, You make me feel so
p-mf
Fm7 F7 B♭ B♭7 B♭7+ E♭maj7 Cm7
spring has sprung, And ev-'ry time I see you grin, I'm such
Dm7 Gm7 C7 F7 B♭ Fdim
a hap-py in-di-vid-u-al. The mo-ment that you speak,

Cm7
F7
B♭
Fdim
Fm7
F7
I wan-na go play hide and seek,
B♭
B♭7
B♭7+
E♭maj7
Cm7
Dm7
Gm7
C7
F7
I wan - na go and bounce the moon, just like a toy bal - loon.
B♭7
B♭dim
B♭7
E♭dim
You and I are
B♭7
B♭dim
Fm7
B♭7
E♭dim
just like a coup-le of tots, run - ning a - cross a
3

Gm7
Bbdim
Eb
Cm
G7
Cm
C7
F7
Cm7
F7
Cb
Bb
mead-ow, pick - ing up lots of for - get - me - nots.
Fdim
Cm7
F7
Bb
Fdim
You make me feel so young.
You make me feel there are
Fm7
F7
Bb
Bb+
Ebmaj7
Ebm
songs to be sung, bells to be rung, and a won - der - ful fling to be
Bb
Dm6
Fdim
Cm7
F7
Bb
Dm6
Fdim
flung.
And e - ven when I'm old and gray,

Cm7
F7
D7+
D7
G7-9
I'm gon-na feel the way I do to - day, 'cause
Cm
G7
Cm
C7
F7
B♭
Gm7
Cm7
F7
F7+
You make me feel so young.
ff
B♭
Gm7
Cm7
F7
F7+
B♭
Gm7
young.
Cm7
F7
F7+
B♭

YOU RAISE ME UP

Words and Music by
ROLF LOVLAND and
BRENDAN GRAHAM

B♭sus
B♭
A♭(9)
E♭2/G
A♭(9)
be, then I am still___ and wait here in the si - lence un - til you
E♭/B♭
B♭7
E♭
Chorus:
Cm
B♭/A♭
A♭
come and sit a while_ with me. You raise me up so I can stand on
cresc.
mf
E♭/G
B♭/D
Cm
B♭/A♭
A♭
E♭/G
B♭
moun - tains.___ You raise_ me up to walk on storm - y___ seas. I am
dim.
mp
E♭
A♭(9)/C
E♭/B♭
E♭/G
A♭(9)
E♭/B♭
B♭7sus
B♭7
E♭
(Violin solo)
strong when I___ am on___ your shoul - ders.___ You raise me up to more than I___ can be.
mf
8vb

F
B♭/F
F
F/A
B♭
Csus
C
B♭(9)/D
B♭
F (9)/A
B♭(9)
F/C
C7sus
F
You raise me
cresc.
Chorus:
Dm
C/B♭
B♭
F/A
C (9)/E
Dm
C/B♭
B♭
up so I can stand on moun - tains. You raise_ me up to walk on storm - y_
f
F/C
Csus
C
F
B♭(9)/D
F/C
F/A
B♭(9)
seas. I am strong when I am on_ your shoul - ders._ You raise me
mf

F/C
C7sus
C7
F
B♭/F
F
up to more than I can be.
You raise me
f
Chorus:
E♭m
D♭/C♭
C♭
G♭/B♭
D♭(9)/F
up so I can stand on moun - tains.
You raise me
E♭m
D♭/C♭
C♭
G♭/D♭
D♭sus
D♭
G♭
C♭
up to walk on storm - y seas.
I am strong when I am on your
G♭
E♭m7
G♭/D♭
D♭7sus
D♭7
G♭
B♭/D
shoul - ders.
You raise me up to more than I can be.
You raise me

E♭m D♭/C♭ C♭ G♭/B♭ D♭(9)/F E♭m D♭/C♭ C♭

up so I can stand on moun - tains. You raise_ me up to walk on storm - y___

G♭/D♭ D♭sus D♭ G♭ C♭ G♭ E♭m7

seas. I am strong when I___ am on___ your shoul - ders.___ You raise me

mf

G♭/D♭ D♭7sus D♭7 E♭m C♭

up to more than I___ can be.___ You raise me

G♭/D♭ D♭7 C♭(9)/G♭ G♭

up to more than I___ can be.___

mp

rit. e dim.

p

YOU'LL NEVER KNOW

Lyrics by
MACK GORDON

Music by
HARRY WARREN

Refrain:

F F/A D♭7/A♭ Gm Gm(maj7) Gm7

1.2. You'll nev - er know just how much I miss you.

Gm Gm7 C7 F/A

You'll nev - er know just how much I care.

F F/A A♭dim7 Gm D7(♭9)

{And if I tried, I still could - n't hide my love for
{You said good - bye, no stars in the sky re - fuse to

Gm
Gm7/C
C7
Gm
Gm7/C
C7/B♭
you.
You ought to know,
for have - n't I told you
shine.
Take it from me,
it's no fun to be a -
F/A
D♭7/A♭
Gm
G7
C7
F
so, a mil - lion or more times?
lone with moon-light and mem - 'ries.
You went a - way and my heart
F/A
D♭7/A♭
Gm
Gm(maj7)
Gm7
went with you.
3
Gm
Gm7
C7
D7
Am7/D
Ddim7
I speak your name in my ev - 'ry prayer.

D7
Ddim7
D7
Gm
D
Gm7(♭5)
If there is some oth - er way to prove that I love you, I
F
A7
Am7(♭5)/E♭
D7
Gm
swear, I don't know how.
You'll nev - er know if you don't
G7
C7
1. F
A♭dim7
Gm7
C7(♯5)
know now.
2. F
D♭7
F6/9
now.

Alfred